Lifting the Mask

your
guide
to
Basel
Fasnacht

by Peter Habicht
illustrations
by Fredy Prack

Bergli Books

Lifting the Mask
your guide to Basel Fasnacht

© 2001 Peter Habicht
illustrations © 2001 Fredy Prack

Published in 2001 and reprinted in 2008 by
Bergli Books Tel.: +41 61 373 27 77
Rümelinsplatz 19 Fax: +41 61 373 27 78
CH-4001 Basel e-mail: info@bergli.ch
Switzerland www.bergli.ch

All rights reserved. No part of this publication may be reproduced, stored in a retrieval system, or transmitted, in any form, or by any means, electronic, mechanical, photocopying, recording or otherwise, without the prior permission in writing from Bergli Books, CH-4001 Basel, Switzerland.

Scans, Pre-press: Oberli Druck, Basel
ISBN 978-3-905252-04-0

For Nadia

Lifting the Mask

Your Guide to Basel Fasnacht:

Prologue
- **About this book** 7
- **What Fasnacht is (and isn't)** 9
- **Fasnacht fever** 13

Morgestraich 15
- **The music** 19
- **Costumes and masks** 25

Monday 35
- **Cortège** 35
- **Cliquen** 39
- **Is Fasnacht funny?** 45
- **Schnitzelbangg** 46

Tuesday 51
- **Kinderfasnacht** 51
- **Lantern Exhibition** 55
- **Guggemuusige** 57

Wednesday 62
- **Organizing Fasnacht (Comité)** 62
- **'Wild' Fasnacht** 64
- **Schyssdräggziigli** 65
- **Gässle** 69
- **The End** 73

History 75

At a glance 87
- **Do's and don'ts** 87
- **More hints** 90
- **What to eat (with recipes)** 91
- **Glossary** 98

Bibliography 107
Index 108
Acknowledgements 116
About the author and the illustrator 117

Peter Habicht

Prologue

About this book

My friend Esther hates Fasnacht. "It's loud. You can't talk to anyone. Pubs and restaurants are cramped and smoky, food is expensive and the service poor. You can't drive into the city center and public transport nearly comes to a standstill..."

All this is quite true. Still, I couldn't agree less. But then, I'm hooked. Or, as we'd say in our local dialect, *aagfrässe*. For me, as for most people in the city of Basel, Fasnacht is the highlight of the year. On the Monday after Ash Wednesday, normal everyday life just stops and everybody joins in what is referred to as *die drey scheenschte Dääg*, the three most beautiful days.

But what, apart from being beautiful, is Fasnacht? Put this question to ten people and you'll get at least ten different answers. Believe me – Fasnacht is so much more than what you see or hear. It is an attitude, a life-style, a passion. Once a year, very early on a wintry Monday morning, a transformation takes place. People get into a state of – what could you call it? – a trance or peaceful bliss that makes them forget about everything else. And this is impossible to put into words.

That's why I never intended to write about it. However, I'll give it a try, because there are many English-

Lifting the Mask

speaking people looking for information about Fasnacht. It seems that during or after the event, visitors storm into bookshops desperate to find out what the hell is (or has been) going on during those days. Others plan to visit Basel for Fasnacht and want to find out about it beforehand. There are a lot of books – but they are written in German or, even more difficult for outsiders, in *Baseldytsch*, the local dialect. It's hard, if not impossible, to find detailed explanations in English.

The main reason for this is that Fasnacht is not a show set-up to attract outside visitors. We do it primarily to please ourselves. "We could do without the tourists" many *Fasnächtler* claim. Maybe – but wouldn't we miss it if there weren't a *Druggede* (an impenetrable crowd) on *Morgestraich* (the beginning event)? Wouldn't it be dull if nobody came to see the big parade on Monday and Wednesday afternoons? And for whom should the *Guggemuusige* (I'll explain who they are later) perform their concerts on Tuesday evening? No, Fasnacht needs an audience and spectators. And the audience is entitled to some basic information.

That's what this book is all about. It is not meant to be an academic study in cultural anthropology – far from it. It is a guidebook to help you enjoy these three special days. In this book you'll find an outline of the course of events from early Monday morning to early Thursday morning. As you read along, you'll learn all about the basics of Fasnacht. For quick reference, check the index at the back of the book and the glossary where the words in dialect are explained.

Fasnacht is always an individual, subjective experience. So is my description. I've been 'doing Fasnacht', as we say, for quite a few years (don't ask how many). Being a piccolo-player (and a 'wild' one), I know more about this aspect of Fasnacht than, say, about Guggemuusige. However, I have tried to look at it through the eyes of the newcomer. I hope that this book covers most of your questions and stimulates your curiosity. But I can't give you a final answer to the very first question, namely, What is Fasnacht? You have to discover the answer yourself. However, let's try to get a first notion.

What Fasnacht is (and isn't)

Fasnacht is a traditional annual festival that takes place in the city of Basel, Switzerland, towards the end of winter or at the beginning of spring (depending on the date of Easter). Fasnacht is the Swiss-German dialect word for carnival. But you will notice that I carefully avoid using the word carnival throughout the book. It is misleading because it makes you think of other carnivals you have seen or heard of, like the famous ones in Rio or Venice, the Mardi Gras in New Orleans or the Karneval in Cologne and Mainz, or indeed the Fasnacht in Lucerne. As you will discover, these comparisons don't work. Fasnacht in Basel is unique.

Nevertheless, I checked my Oxford dictionary where carnival is the "public merrymaking and feasting, usually with processions of persons in fancy dress, especially in Roman Catholic countries during the week before Lent." To begin with, Basel isn't particularly in a Roman Catholic region. It's primarily a Protestant city. We celebrate Fasnacht not before, but during the first week of Lent after all the other carnivals are over. Our Fasnacht is merry, but it is not as frolicsome as in other places. Quite the contrary! There is gravity about Fasnacht that astonishes all first-time visitors. It may be loud, colorful and funny – but there is also a strange melancholy and a certain solemnity. Excessive drinking, for instance, is not the point. You'll never find a true Fasnächtler drunk during these days (well... maybe there are a few exceptions).

I think it is the mixture of seriousness and lightness that makes the Basel Fasnacht so unique. There are some things you can compare to other

Lifting the Mask

carnivals. There's lots of music (but no dancing). There's a big parade, too. And we do wear fancy dress. And this is where the likeness to the dictionary definition ends. A costume alone is not enough. We also wear a mask.

Every year some eager tourists come to Basel with preconceived ideas about Fasnacht. They have nice costumes, paint their faces and wear, say, a funny hat or a wig and think they can join the party. I can give you only one word of advice: don't.

Fasnacht is not the everybody-join-in kind of event. Of course, everybody is welcome to come and observe the happenings. But there is a strict division between those taking an active part and those who watch. Participants either play one of the traditional instruments, the drum or the piccolo. Or they march in front of the bands, clearing the way. Others play in one of the big brass bands called Guggemuusige. And all of them have to know about countless little do's and don'ts. There are no written rules, but a behavioral code that we pick up in the beginning of our Fasnacht career.

If you don't know about these rules, it is much wiser just to watch what's going on. I promise you that this is fun too. More than 20,000 participants (and that's a low esti-

Peter Habicht

mate) provide a festival for your senses that you are not likely ever to forget. And luckily, there are only a few rules for on-lookers. You'll find them on page 87. Observe these and you'll be fine.

Fasnachtsfieber (Fasnacht fever)

Officially, Fasnacht lasts for three days (and nights). But if you live in the region of Basel, you can feel a rising tension from, say, Christmas onward. By then, preparations are well on the way: masks and costumes are being made, the lantern-painters set down to work. There is a word for this happy expectancy: *Fasnachtsfieber* (Fasnacht fever). The closer the big moment draws, the higher the temperature gets. In the month before Fasnacht, there is a big show called the *Drummeli* staged by the *Comité* (the organizing board of Fasnacht). Similar shows with drum and piccolo-music, *Schnitzelbängg* and sketches (*Rahmestiggli*) are staged by several small theaters. In some outskirts of the city (Lange Erlen, Allschwilerwald, Bruderholz) you may hear the Cliques and *Gugge* bands rehearsing their marches. The fever keeps rising.

Fasnacht fever reaches its peak on Sunday evening, when the Cliques carry their lanterns to their respective

Lifting the Mask

starting points. This lovely tradition is called *Ladäärne yypfyffe* (to pipe the lantern in). The gigantic lanterns are still covered and, as the expression implies, they are accompanied only by the piccolo-players in plain clothes. It isn't Fasnacht yet; but it's so very close...

After that, everybody goes home and tries to get some sleep. This is very hard, if not impossible, because Fasnacht starts in the middle of that night, or rather *very* early in the morning. So many don't go to bed at all (restaurants and pubs are open all night). As a participant you know that you need all the rest you can get (be it ever so little) to help you get through the next three days. A common nightmare is, of course, that you will oversleep and miss Morgestraich. But the multitude of alarm clocks you set will get you out of bed in time. The city slowly begins to fill with people already at 2 a.m. Normally, it is bitter cold – so be sure to have warm clothes. Everything is rather quiet, although the whole town is seething with anticipation. Men and women in costumes holding their masks in their arms hurry to the meeting places of their Cliques. There they hang around, blow on their frozen fingers and wait for the big moment.

Morgestraich

The beginning is spectacular. Morgestraich, a kind of pre-dawn bugle-call or tattoo, starts at 4 a.m. sharp. You wouldn't believe the number of people that are crammed in the streets and squares of the center of town. Just before 4 a.m. there's an excited hush. Then you hear the church bells chime. At the last stroke, all the streetlights go out. For a split second, everything is quiet (except for some tourists going "oooh" and "aaah"). Then you hear the shouted commands: "*Morgestraich... vorwärts... marsch!*"

The next instant everything is drowned in the high-pitched melodies of the piccolos and the beating of the drums. Gigantic painted lanterns (*Ladäärne*) glow in the night. Smaller lanterns, the so-called *Stäggeladäärne*, are carried on long poles. And there are thousands of small *Kopfladäärne* (head lanterns) that the musicians have fixed on top of their masks. The bands start pushing their way slowly through the crowd. They are assisted by the indispensable *Vordraab* (vanguards) who are also masked but are not playing instruments. They march in front of the Clique and clear the way which can be a very hard job indeed.

These first moments never fail to give everybody goose-pimples, leaving you speechless and spellbound. Even to those who have experienced it many times, Morgestraich never loses its magic. This explosion of color

Lifting the Mask

and sound is the beginning of Fasnacht and the main highlight (or one of the highlights). As a Fasnächtler, you wouldn't miss it for the world.

After the first hour or so, the crowds begin to thin out. People swarm into restaurants to get the traditional Morgestraich breakfast: flour soup and onion tart. Try it. It is not as revolting as it sounds. (See the recipes on pages 92 to 98.)

Nobody hangs around in the restaurants for long. Others want a seat as well – and Fasnacht is taking place outside. After warming up indoors, you won't feel the cold air so much. Just keep walking around town observing the many processions of musicians and plunge right into this trance-like state of existence only Fasnacht provides.

At daybreak, people begin to go home – and back to bed. They want to be fit and ready for the big parade in the afternoon.

Morgestraich takes place in the entire city center. Each Clique starts from a different place – so, as a spectator, you don't have to be at a particular spot. Because of the crowds, I recommend you avoid the big squares and streets like Marktplatz or Freie Strasse. These are the busiest spots – but only go there if you want to experience what claustrophobia really is. If you don't like being squeezed and pushed around in a mass of bodies, go, for example, to Martinskirche or Leonhardskirche, where the smaller Cliques start. It is (slightly) less crowded and more romantic.

The Music

The traditional instruments of Fasnacht are drums and fifes (or, rather, piccolos). The tunes we play are marching songs. It is as bad as that. For three days (and countless hours of practising during the year) everybody, even the greatest pacifist, happily plays what was originally military music. The Morgestraich march itself is an old assembly call of the Swiss army. And we don't only play these marches – we love them. We hum them softly when we hear them practiced during the year. And inadvertently we fall into that peculiar ambling gait of (about) ninety steps a minute that carries us around during the three days of Fasnacht.

Some say people in Basel are born with drums. Of course this is unlikely since a typical Basel drum weighs about eleven pounds. It is made of a metal cylinder of 40 cm (about 15 inches) height and roughly the same diameter.

Lifting the Mask

The drum skin is nowadays of plastic, which is more weather-resistant than the lambskins used previously. It has a high, metallic sound and is fastened with leather straps around the drummer's shoulders (the straps are usually hidden by the costume).

It is truly amazing how many drummers there are – and how skilfully they play, because drumming isn't easy. It takes about three to five years to learn to play it well (and life-long practicing afterwards). It's said you have to start learning it when you're young or you'll never grasp how to do it properly. This art is taught by the Cliques themselves. Each has a school, the so-called 'young guard', where special instructors teach children about drumming, about playing the piccolo, and about Fasnacht in general. The high level of musical skills achieved at Fasnacht is thanks to these schools.

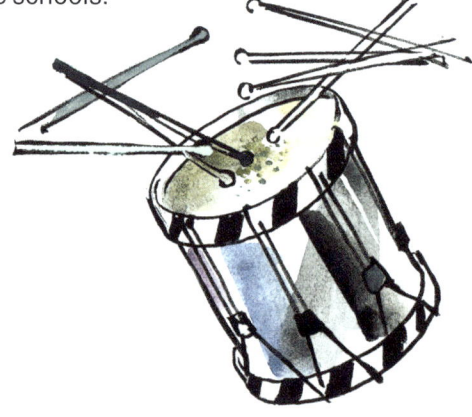

Until not so long ago, drumming used to be the domain of boys. Even today, there are some chauvinists in a few all-male Cliques who maintain that "girls can't drum" (small wonder; they refuse to teach them). But evidence is against them. The girls are catching up.

However, most of the girls (and, as for that, the boys) prefer to learn the other 'traditional' instrument, the piccolo. Maybe this is because it is much easier to play. Even the not-so-musically-gifted can learn it in a year or two. (It is torture to live in the neighbourhood of somebody making his or her first attempts. The piccolo is high-pitched, loud and very piercing.) And, whereas the drummers have to carry a heavy burden, the piccolo player's instrument weighs only about four ounces.

You will notice that the Basel piccolo is different from a regular concert piccolo which looks more or less like a small flute (hence the name: *piccolo* is the Italian word for small). The Basel piccolo has a combination of holes and keys and is much easier to play. It was specially developed during the 20th century. It acquired its definite shape only in the 1960s – and only then did it become the number one Fasnacht instrument. Today there are about 10,000 piccolo-players in Basel. Can you imagine any other city in the world where more than 6% of the population play the same musical instrument?

Of course, there was a kind of a small flute before that. After all, drums and fifes are very old instruments. We hear of drums and fifes being played in Basel as early as the Middle Ages. But they were not associated with Fasnacht. They were military instruments, played when the mercenaries went to war. Or played when the guilds paraded on their festival days, namely for inspections of their arms. This is, by the way, one of the roots of today's Fasnacht (see the chapter on history page 75).

Peter Habicht

When Fasnacht began to shape into what it is today, the fifes had almost disappeared. In the first half of the 20th century, the drum was the main Fasnacht instrument. The bands had only a few pipers who played a small number of marches in only one voice. Today, all marches have been arranged for three voices at least. This shows that the music has changed considerably along with the instrument itself. And it is still changing.

Lifting the Mask

A hundred years ago, there were only a couple of Swiss and French military marches. These are still played: *die Alte*, for instance, is highly popular. It is usually the first march everybody learns. Later, British and American marches were added. That's why you may hear familiar tunes like 'Scotland the Brave' (in a march called *Whisky*), 'Rule Britannia' (*d'Brite*), 'The British Grenadiers' (*Arabi*) and many more.

In the 1960s and 1970s, the marches became more melodious. For example, elements of baroque music were integrated (*Altfrangg*, *Barogg*). Still, they were all set to an easy key, G-major, D-major or, occasionally, C-major. And all tunes that were borrowed were adapted to the same measure, the 2/4-time (with the occasional rhythmic change to 6/8-time.) Now, the music is changing again. New tricky harmonies appear – and there are attempts to change the measure. However, the first march with a 'jazzy' swing, *s Nunnefirzli*, took more than ten years to be broadly accepted. But who knows? In twenty years or so we may skip and bounce around to a completely different sound.

However, I don't think the old favourites will disappear yet. Today there are more than two hundred marches and new ones are written every year. You can't memorize them all (you can't carry the notes around with you, so you have to know your marches by heart). The average repertoire of a Clique consists of about 25 marches. There are new fancy ones, but always some of the so-called 'classics' too. This way we can easily split our groups (this usually happens on Tuesday) and mix with others and always be able to find some tunes to play together.

Costumes and masks

The mask is, apart from the instruments, the most important accessory of Fasnacht. Every participant wears one – along with the costume, of course. Mask and costume are designed to match. You can't wear the one without the other. Incidentally, the dialect word *Massge* (mask) is only used for the whole outfit. The mask itself is called *Larve*, or, lovingly, *dr Kopf* (the head), which underlines its importance. Putting on your mask is part of the transformation that takes place during Fasnacht. Life behind the mask is different.

The variety of motifs is simply astounding. Masks come in all shapes and colors. Some are funny, some frightening, and some melancholic – but all of them are fascinating. There is no limit to the imagination. You see all kinds of animals (e.g. birds, cows, pigs), witches, clowns, monks and so on.

Lifting the Mask

There are also some traditional masks. Many of these derive from an old European theater tradition, the Commedia dell'Arte, like the *Harlekin* (harlequin or *Arlequino*) or the *Bajass* (Bajazzo). Up to the middle of the 20th century, historical soldiers' uniforms were highly popular. But nowadays, figures like the *Altfrangg* (an old uniform of the Prussian army) or the *Stänzler* (the old city guard of Basel) have practically disappeared.

A vast majority of the masks are made of papier-mâché. Some people make their masks themselves. All you

Peter Habicht

need is clay, plaster, paste, paper and a lot of patience. You make a clay mould first, cast it in plaster, lay out the resulting negative with strips of paper and cardboard that have been dipped in paste. You take it out when it's dry, cut the holes for peeping through, paint and varnish it. I'm no hand at making masks (I have tried). So I prefer buying my masks in a specialized shop. There are many of them, and it is really fun to visit one. The walls are all covered with various masks. They are all white. The artist will fix the one you have chosen to your head by means of a close-fitting papier-mâché cap called a *Güpfi*, check where to cut the holes for the eyes and the mouth, then add a mane of straw hair or a hat (or whatever) and paint the mask in colors that match your costume.

As a Fasnächtler, you don't have just one costume, but several. You'll have one for cold weather, one for a warm Fasnacht. You'll have one with a little lantern for Morgestraich, another one for Tuesday when each member of a Clique has free choice of costume (this way of dressing is called *Charivari*). And every year, each Fasnächtler gets a new costume to wear at the big parades on Monday and Wednesday when members of the Cliques have costumes designed for the *Sujet* (theme) the Clique is performing: one design for all the drummers, another for the piccolo-players.

Some traditional costumes and masks

Waggis

The *Waggis* is easily the best-known figure of Fasnacht. His mask has a huge mouth with large teeth, an enormous nose and a shock of yellow hair. He wears wooden clogs and a costume of white trousers, a blue shirt and a red handkerchief knotted around the neck. Nowadays, the colors vary. The costume (and the hair of the mask) can be green, purple or whatever color. But the traditional ones point to the origin of this figure. Blue, white and red are the colors of the French flag. Indeed, the Waggis was, in the beginning, a (quite nasty) parody of the Alsatian farmers who, in the old days, sold their produce on the open street-market in Basel. It is interesting to notice that Waggis is still the correct, if almost forgotten, dialect word for Alsatians. But nowadays, people aren't referring to their neighbors across the border when they say Waggis, but to the Fasnacht figure. The meaning has shifted from the original to the parody.

A Waggis is very loud and rude and above all playful, looking for a good time or for trouble, or sometimes both. He'll point his finger at you, shout at you, stuff you with *Räppli* (confetti) and throw oranges all over the place. He drags strange things (for example a huge bone on a leash)

Lifting the Mask

around with him. His happiest time is Monday and Wednesday afternoons, when he is, at least for the children, the unchallenged hero of the parade. But you can also meet him late at night, when he strolls around town in search of potential victims for his pranks.

Alti Dante

This figure is the parody of the old spinster. She has a thin, pointed nose, an old fashioned wig and usually wears a straw hat with a large brim the way they were fashionable about 150 years ago. Similarly old-fashioned is her

elegant gown and the tiny woven or knitted handbag called the *ridicule* (reticule).

There's no telling who's hiding behind an Alti Dante (or any other costume). Don't be surprised if the group of costumed women you observed parading in the street take off their masks in the restaurant and reveal themselves to be bearded and bald-headed men.

Ueli

His ancestor is the old medieval fool or jester. He has a big hooked nose and two large (textile) horns protruding

Lifting the Mask

from his mask. His costume is covered with tiny bells chiming brightly at every step. It is, apart from the Waggis, probably the best-loved of the traditional costumes. By the way, Ueli is the dialect form of Ulrich and is (or rather has been) a very popular first name given to boys born in Basel.

Blätzlibajass

This is one of the traditional characters taken from the Commedia dell'Arte. It's the Bajazzo, whose name derived from the Italian word *pagliaccio* (sack of straw), an allusion to his sack-like outfit. Originally, the Blätzlibajass

Peter Habicht

costume was covered with rag patches sewn on like shingles. They are nowadays replaced by hundreds of small, tile-shaped tabs of felt. They also cover his long, cone-shaped hat. Can you imagine how time-consuming it must be to sew all these tiles (*Blätzli*) to an old overall? But all these pieces of cloth or felt make a very warm costume – ideal for a cold Fasnacht.

Harlekin

Another character from the Commedia dell'Arte can easily be spotted thanks to his broad Venetian hat.

Dummpeeter

It's not quite clear where he comes from – or what his name means. Some say it derives from Drumpeter (trumpeter), because he (traditionally) has a tiny brass trumpet hanging round his neck. Others maintain that his name means 'silly Peter' (*dumm* = stupid) because of his complexion. Indeed, he has a dreamy, naive look, a snub-nose and a white pigtail matching his 18th-century attire.

Pierrot

This figure's great-grandfather was a Commedia dell'Arte figure too. But he came to us via French pantomime theater (pierrot = little Peter). He has a slightly arrogant and melancholic look and a peacock's feather on top of his round cap.

Monday

Cortège (The Parade)

Monday morning after Morgestraich is quiet. Some people go to work, though most offices are closed. But the shops are open until noon. However, most Fasnächtler are resting. They're all back early in the afternoon for the big parade. The *Cortège,* as we call it, starts at 1.30 p.m. and follows a circular route from Marktplatz to Barfüsserplatz, up Steinenberg towards the Museum of Fine Arts (Kunstmuseum), over Wettsteinbrücke to Kleinbasel and past Claraplatz and Mittlere Brücke back to Marktplatz. It doesn't really matter where you go. The same show is everywhere. Personally, I like the bridges best, because you get a nice view of the river and the old town as well as of the parade itself.

Another recommendable spot is the corner of Barfüsserplatz and Steinenberg, where you get a good survey of the groups coming downhill. Or, indeed, going uphill. The parade is so big that the participants circulate in two directions. If you stand between them, you often don't know which way to look. Whatever, you're bound to miss something happening on the other side. But you have a second chance: Wednesday afternoon, the parade is repeated (same time, same place). Even then, I doubt that you'll be able to take in everything there is to see.

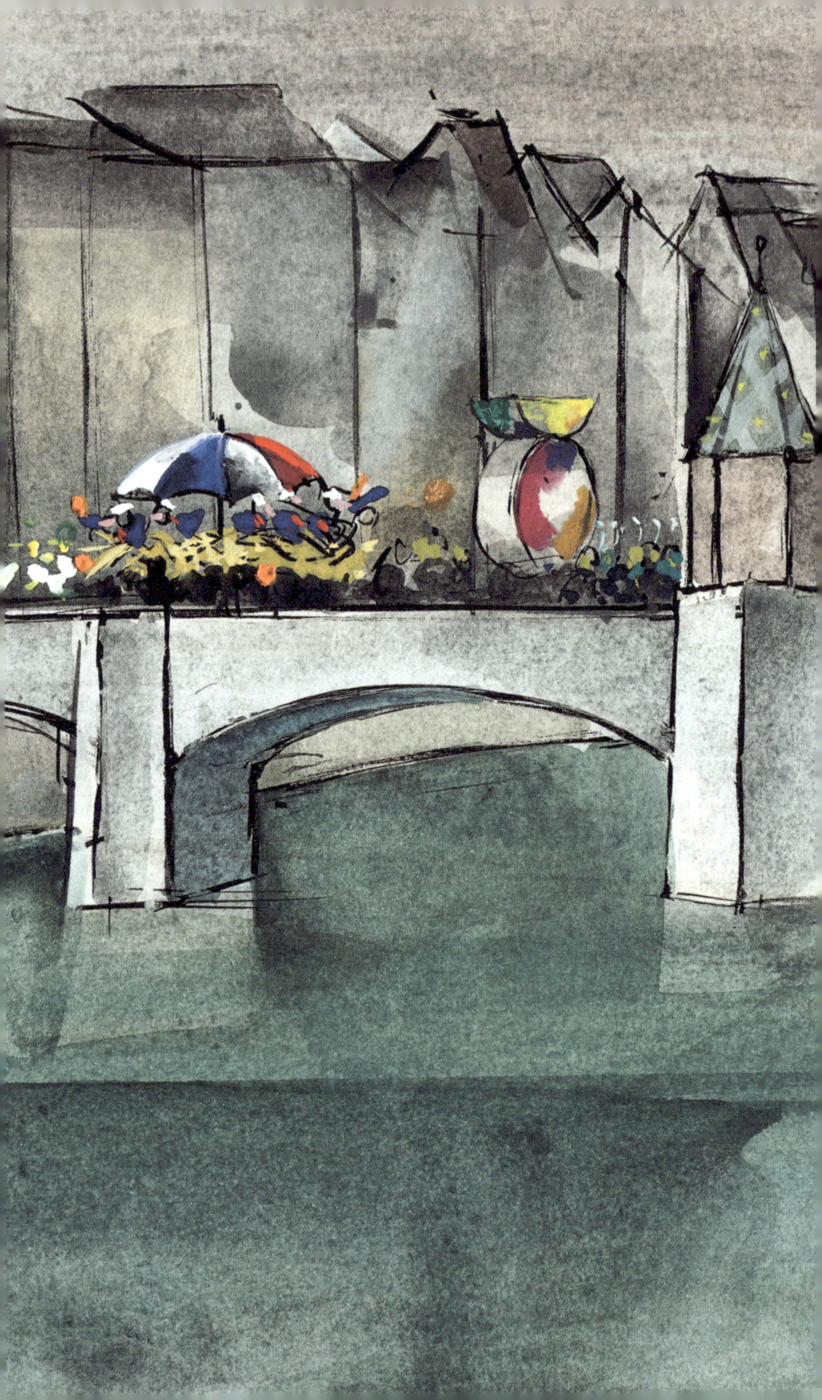

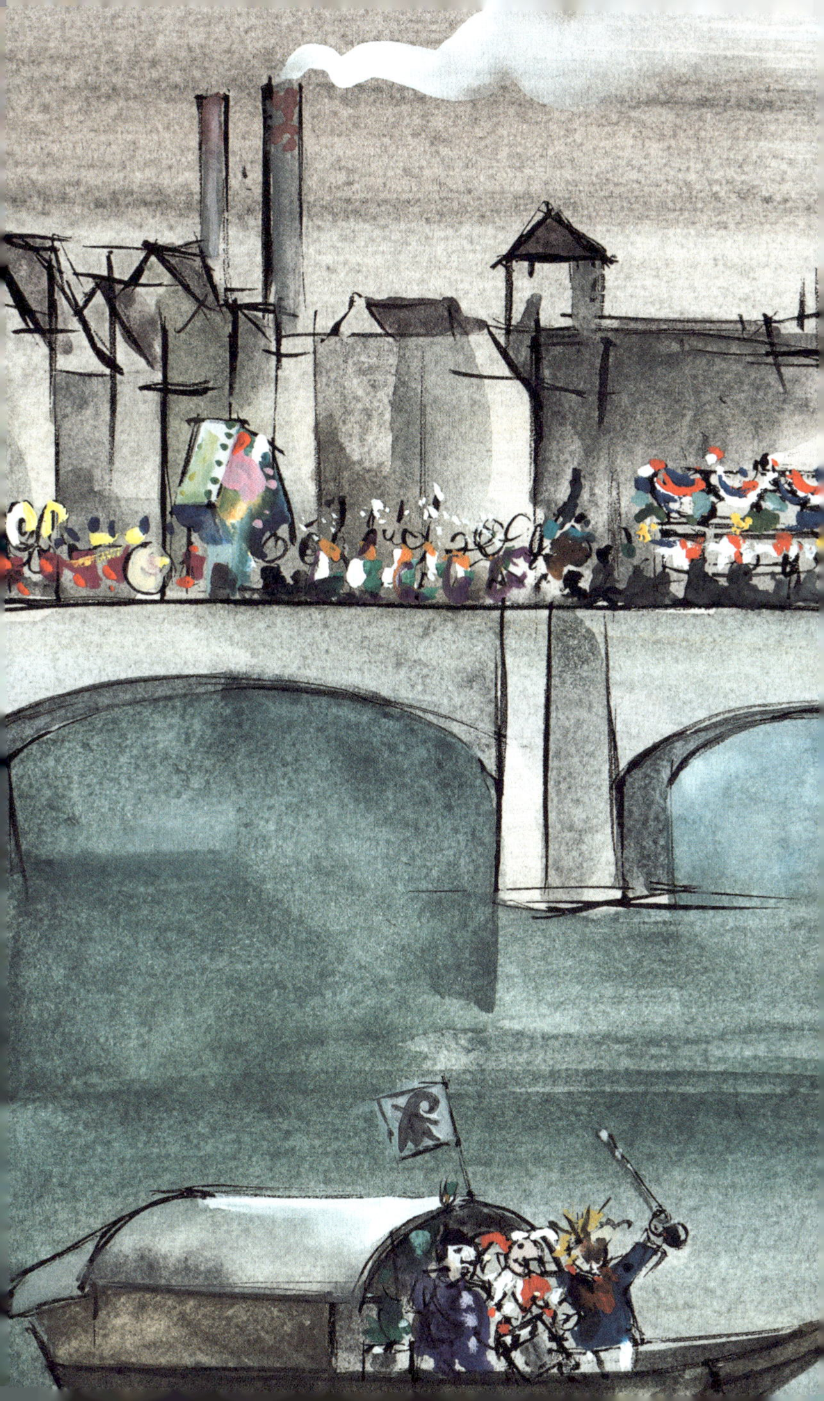

Lifting the Mask

Until nightfall, thousands of masked people parade in front of you. You'll be entranced (and dazzled) by the enormous variety of costumes and masks, of colors and music. The spectacle that unfolds in front of your eyes is quite different from what you experienced early in the morning. For atmosphere, of course, you can't beat Morgestraich. But then, Morgestraich doesn't change much. Usually, people wear the same costume year after year. This certainly isn't the case with the Cortège where everything is brand new and designed just for the occasion. The creative energy that goes into the parade is unbelievable. For this moment, hundreds of people have been working for months. Now, the Cliques proudly present their theme or Sujet to a vast audience.

There is another difference. On Morgestraich, only drums and piccolos were to be heard. Now, there are also many big brass bands: the so-called *Guggemuusige* (or just *Gugge*). They play deliberately off-tune – a crazy, swinging sound that contrasts to the solemn marching music of the Cliques. I'll tell you more about them later.

In addition to the Cliques and the Gugge, you'll see more than a hundred big decorated *Wääge* (wagons or floats) pulled by tractors. They transport the highly popular Waggis who hand out sweets and toys to the kids, throw oranges at you (don't throw them back!) and shower (or stuff) you with confetti. Beware! They want to tempt you to get closer so they can cram confetti down your back. But they might (I said might!) also present you with carnations or the beautiful yellow-flowered mimosas – so don't run too far.

And you'll see another Fasnacht character, too: the Alti Dante. She is, of course, much more sophisticated than the rough Waggis. She doesn't ride on a decorative wagon. Instead, she sits in beautiful old horse-drawn carriage: the *Chaise*. From there, she gracefully hands out sweets to the children and flowers (roses, mostly) to a selected few.

The Gugge, Wääge and Chaise add a colorful, happy note to the parade. However, the pillars of the Fasnacht are the big Cliques of drummers and piccolo-players. Let's turn our attention to them.

Cliquen

To begin with, a Clique is nothing but an association or a club. We Swiss do love clubs to organize and structure our hobbies. A club in Switzerland has written statutes, endless meetings, a managing board and the contest of who's to be burdened with finances and who's to be honoured with the presidency. A Clique is not that different from other clubs. What is different is its purpose, namely to prepare and perform Fasnacht together and to hold up Tradition (notice the capital T). Besides, the Cliques are also strong personal networks and play an important role in the social life of this city.

A Clique is often a large organisation with many more members than you can actually see in costumes in the parades. They have countless 'passive' members who help prepare the big event. A Clique usually has three or four sections. There's the so-called *Jungi Garde* (young guard), where the junior generation is introduced to the art of Fasnacht. There's the main group called the *Stamm*. And there's the *Alti Garde* (old guard), where members of ages 40 upwards enjoy Fasnacht at a more leisurely pace. Some Cliques have a special section for women, whereas in others, genders are mixed. It has to be mentioned that there are still some men-only associations. What's more: they're even proud of it . . .

There are more than two hundred Cliques in Basel. But only about 40 who entertain a Jungi Garde (which includes a school for drumming and piccolo-playing) count as *Stammclique*. They are all well-known and sought out in the parade, because they usually put up the biggest show. Each of them has its own traditions and an unmistakable individual style.

Members of a Clique get together regularly throughout the year. The meetings usually take place in a restaurant or the clubhouses called *Cliquekäller* (Clique cellar). During Fasnacht, some of the Cliquekäller are open to the public. They are marked with a small lantern at the entrance. If you see one, go inside. The atmosphere is brilliant.

After Easter holidays, the pipers and drummers of a Clique start rehearsing their marches in groups. In autumn, a special committee sits down to discuss, debate and decide about the *Sujet* of next year's Fasnacht. As the word indicates, the Sujet is the subject or theme the Clique is 'playing' (lampooning) on Fasnacht. Given its importance, the choice of the theme is a matter of deep consideration. After all, it has to be transposed into eye-catching images and satirical verses. Once the question is settled, the Clique's artists (every Clique has its own) get busy. Costumes and masks are designed, the lantern-painter provides the first sketches, and the Clique's poet sets to work on the *Zeedel* (see next paragraph). Most of the handiwork, like the making of the masks and the sewing of the costumes, is done by professionals. But there are still some Cliques where the members themselves do a lot of the work. Slowly but surely, the Fasnacht appearance of the Clique's theme begins to take shape. And Fasnacht fever

Lifting the Mask

sets in. To the insider, Fasnacht doesn't start on Morgestraich, but much earlier. For some, it never stops.

Let us return to the parade. From the Clique's point of view, this is the highlight of Fasnacht. Here they have a platform to present their Sujet. The whole *Zug*, as we call the marching entity of a Clique, is dedicated to it. (Like so many Fasnacht expressions, Zug is a military term meaning a platoon). The Vordraab marches in front and hands out long strips of paper (*Zeedel*) on which the Sujet is explained in a satirical poem (the Zeedel poems are written in the Basel dialect, so you're not the only one who may not understand them. Most visitors from Germany won't either). In bigger Cliques, a member of the Vordraab drags a small wagon with one or several artistically arranged objects: the *Requisit*. This weird sculpture is one of the means to visualize the theme. Behind the Requisit follows the heart and the centerpiece of every Zug: the huge, colorful lantern. On it, the Sujet is illustrated in a big caricature.

Behind the lantern follow the pipers and the drummers. The most impressive figure amongst them is the *Tambourmajor*, the drum major. He wears a mask that is much bigger than everybody else's. This over-sized figure represents yet another commentary on the Sujet. With his long staff the drum major conducts the drummers as they are marching along and majestically salutes the audience.

A Zug could be described as a single work of art in several parts, a living 'tableau' or a 'Gesamtkunstwerk' that passes in front of your eyes. Please don't disturb it, for example by trying to sneak through the gap between the pipers and the drummers. It is very irritating for the musicians. If you want to cross the street, wait till the whole Clique has passed by you.

What kinds of topics are likely to become the Sujet of a Clique? Well, anything, really. Never forget that Fasnacht is an important outlet for letting off steam. Happenings of everyday life are critically commented on or made fun of. Trifles can just as well become a Sujet as serious matters. Let me give you an example. Recently, many Cliques made fun of a fund-raising plastic duck-race on the Rhine – certainly not an event that changes the world. In the same year, another Clique, dressed up as pigs, presented a profound criticism of the rising ruthlessness in our society.

Anything that has drawn public attention during the year can (and, indeed, does) become a Sujet. Local themes, of course, are the favorites. The city's government, for instance, is an evergreen. So is the local soccer club, the FC Basel, or the public transport system. Swiss politics, too, will always provide suitable subjects for satire. Other targets are, for example, church matters, a recent election in America, or themes like the computerisation of the world and so on. There's a wide range of possibilities, and you will rarely see the same topics again and again. It does happen, of course, that two or more Cliques 'play' the same Sujet. But then, it is fascinating to compare their interpretations.

Anyway, the interesting question is not so much what is represented, but how it is done. It is surprising how far the satire actually goes. In other places, it would probably keep the law-courts busy. Here, it is not only accepted, but appreciated. We do show our teeth at Fasnacht. And we do it in our own peculiar way; a way, that is, in the rest of Switzerland, generally referred to as 'the Basel sense of humor'.

Peter Habicht

Is Fasnacht funny?

This seems a very strange question indeed. But it is justified, because many visitors are really puzzled by just how *serious* the whole event is. Fasnacht is never as frivolous as other carnivals. Instead, you can feel a certain solemnity or gravity to it, even a bittersweet melancholic touch. But don't let this fool you. It is also very, very funny.

But, alas, the texts on the lanterns, the Zeedel and the Schnitzelbängg (explained below) are in a dialect that you may not be able to understand. There are many play-on-words and little verbal puns that are impossible to translate. And the Fasnacht humor requires a lot of background information. I refrain from giving you an example, because, as you know, a joke is only funny when told, not when explained. However, I will attempt to describe the Basel humor in general and at Fasnacht in particular.

In this city people are not only born with drums, as the saying goes, but also with a very sharp tongue. For this, we are known (and respected) all over Switzerland. Our sharp tongues need exercise. And Fasnacht is the ideal platform for that. Here, we learn about it when we grow up. The result is that the whole city shares a similar sense of humor unparalleled in Switzerland or in other German-speaking countries. Incidentally, it is pretty close to 'British humour'. Basel humor is never (or hardly ever) crude and blatant. Ideally, it is of the intelligent kind: witty, sophisticated – and (ever so often) very black. There are limits, of course. But they are hard to define. Somehow, by mutual consent, the limits are known and respected. It is surprisingly rare that a joke hits below the belt.

I admit that all this is slightly over-enthusiastic. Not everybody who tries to be funny actually is. What I mean to say is that the Fasnächtler *understands* this particular kind of humor. And there are many who are able to produce it. Let's turn to those masters of Fasnacht humor we haven't met so far: the Schnitzelbänggler. They make their appearances on Monday and Wednesday evenings after the parade. Their stage isn't the street, but the packed, smoke-filled restaurants.

The Schnitzelbangg

Isn't this a beautiful tongue twister? Try another one: The plural of Schnitzelbangg is Schnitzelbängg. Those who sing Schnitzelbängg are Schnitzelbänggler. Everything clear?

Schnitzelbänggler are people who sing funny verses to (preferably) popular tunes. The Schnitzelbangg-verses

Peter Habicht

are best compared to limericks. They have (or should have) a punch line. Each verse (*Vääars*) is accompanied by a drawing (*Helge*) that illustrates the verse without giving away the joke. After their performance, Schnitzelbänggler hand out Zeedel (strips of paper) with the verses printed on them.

The Schnitzelbängg are extremely popular. The 'stage' names of many of these groups are well known but nobody is supposed to know who's really hiding behind the masks. The best verses are quoted long after Fasnacht is over, some even for years. And though they are broadcast on radio and TV, nothing can replace the live-experience. Small wonder that the restaurants are crammed. In many places, you have to book a table months in advance.

The Schnitzelbangg is an art form only few can master (although there are many who try). A Schnitzelbänggler has to be well informed about local (and other) events. He or she keeps combing through news items and events throughout the year. A good Schnitzelbänggler develops a talent for a surprising twist and for an unexpected punch line. Apart from this, a Schnitzelbänggler needs a good voice and a gift for putting on a good performance. A lot of stamina is needed too, for on Monday and Wednesday evening their timetables are just packed.

There are about a hundred of them. They come as one-man-shows, in pairs or in groups of three or four. The

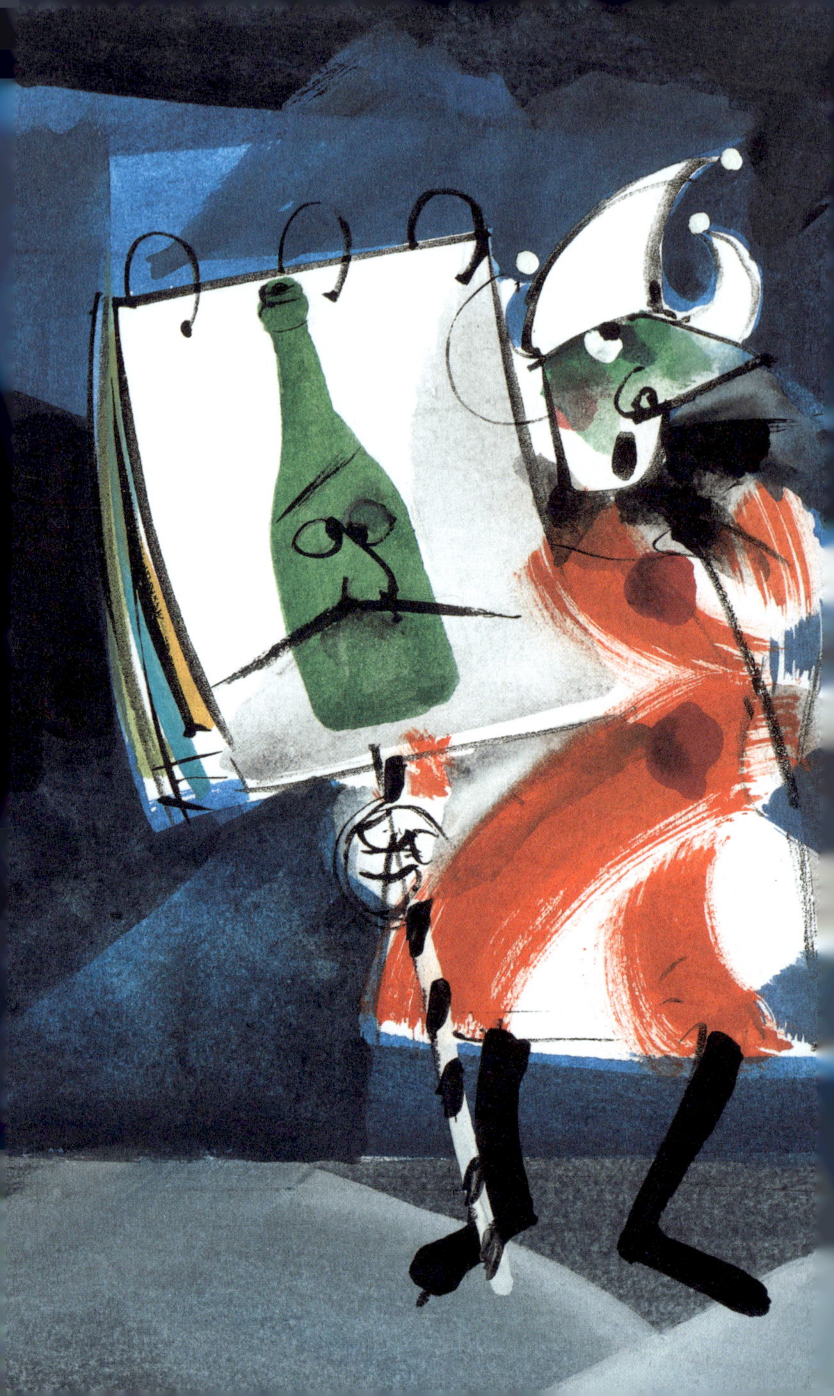

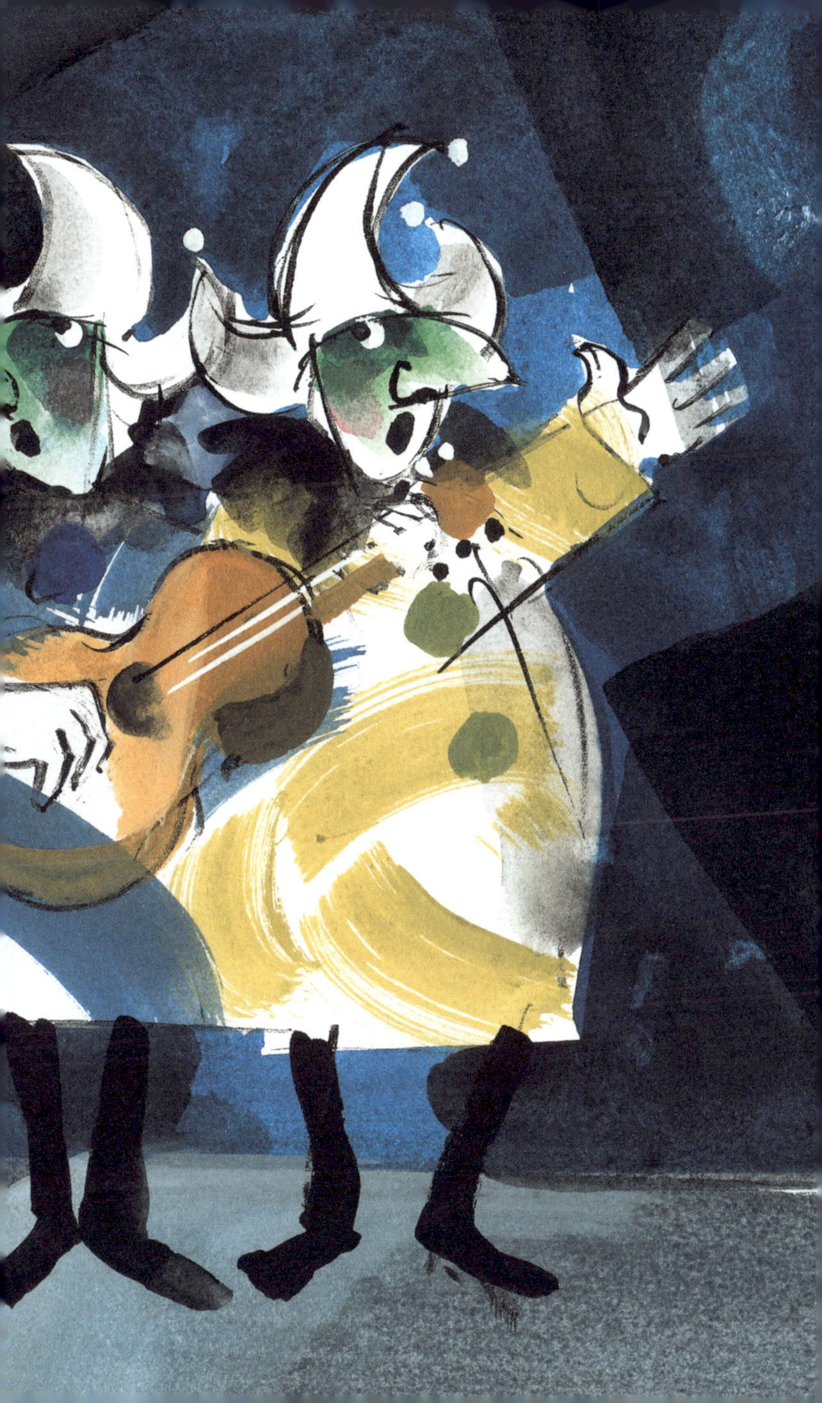

majority is organized in one of the Schnitzelbangg-organisations, of which the Schnitzelbangg-Comité is generally considered to be the best. But there are also quite a few unorganized (or 'wild') groups. They prefer choosing their own places and times to perform. Unlike their organised colleagues, they don't have to hurry from restaurant to restaurant with their guitars or harmonicas, their Helge and their Zeedel and be forever behind schedule.

Tuesday

Twenty or thirty years ago, Tuesday was not an official day of Fasnacht. Most people went back to work and the shops were open as on a normal weekday. During the day at least, things seemed to be (almost) normal.

This has changed considerably. Today, it may be the favorite of the three days (at least for the insider). True – there's no Clique activity or scheduled parade route. But is this a reason for staying at home? Certainly not! As a Fasnächtler, you put on your Tuesday's costume, grab your instrument and march about town for hours on end. Alone. Or in small groups. Or, indeed, with your family. For Tuesday, more than any other day, is the big day for the kids.

Kinderfasnacht (children's carnival)

Most of us were first exposed to that highly contagious and life-inflicting virus called Fasnacht on a Tuesday afternoon. In the beginning we were in our mother's arms or on our daddy's shoulders. Later we sat in a rack-wagon (a small copy of the *Waggiswääge*) or drummed with two sticks on a cardboard box while marching proudly along with our parents. Later still, at the age of eight or so, we became members of a young guard and learned about Fasnacht, its music and traditions. (Not every career is the same. My parents, for instance, were not Fasnächtler at all.

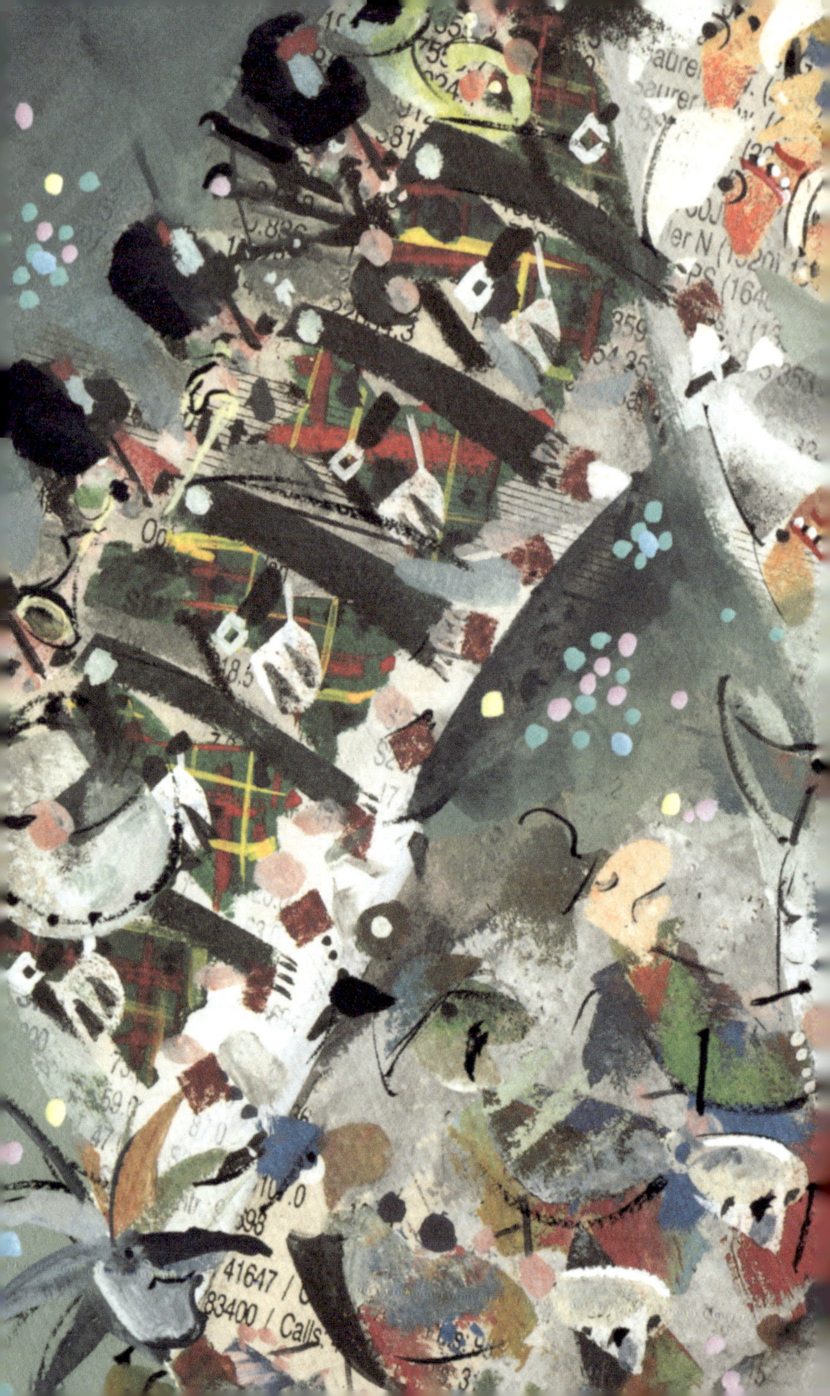
41647 /
83400 / Calls

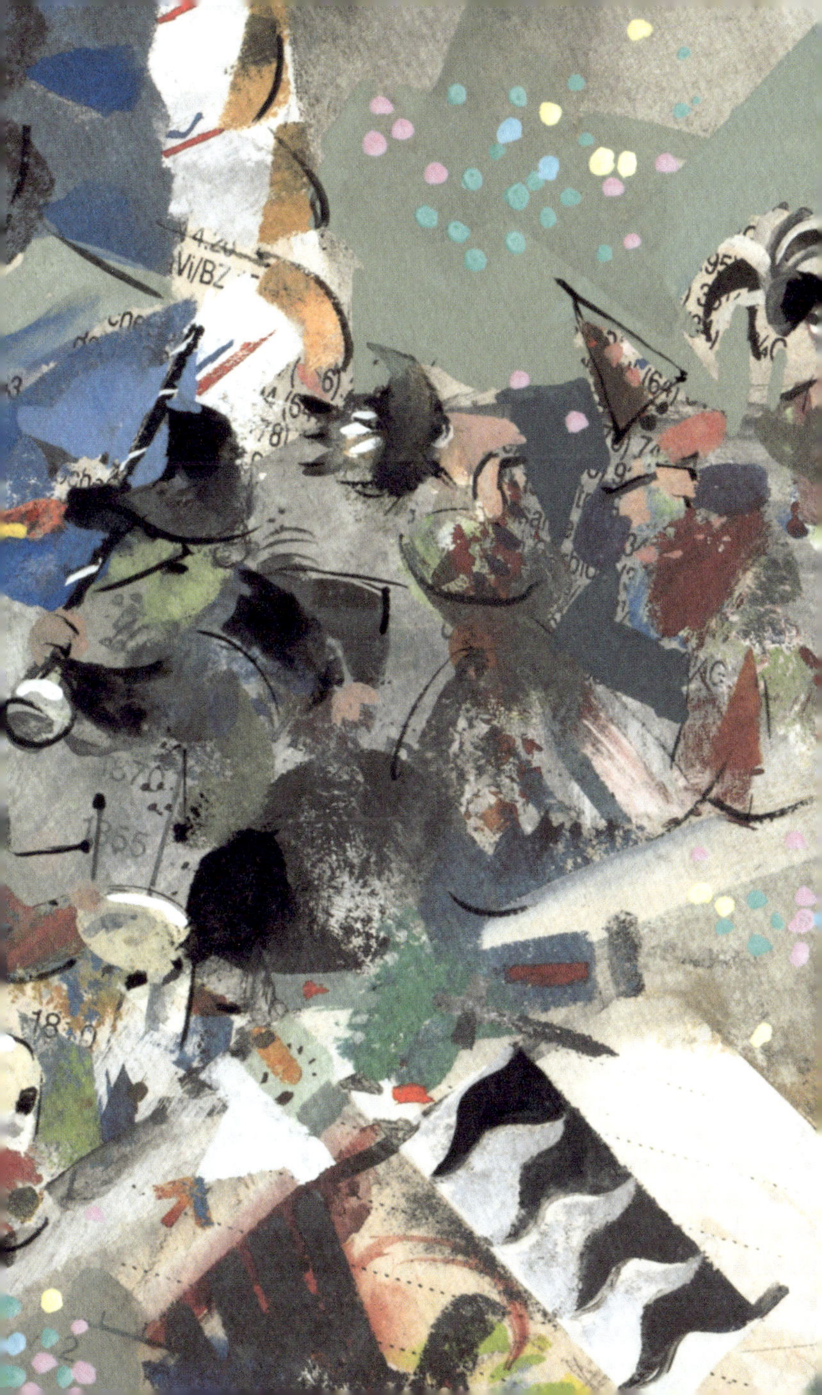

They sent me off to the mountains skiing. But to no avail. The virus got me later.)

Fasnacht Tuesday brings back all these memories. No wonder people have the tendency to get slightly sentimental about it. But even if you don't have these memories, Tuesday afternoon will not fail to enchant you. They're all there. Toddlers, clutching their mummy's leg, taking everything in with big round eyes. Small kids in their wagons throwing sweets or (preferably) confetti, shrieking with delight while their elder brothers and sisters have a go at playing their first marches on their newly acquired piccolos or drums. They try to keep in pace with mom and dad, who are (finally) 'off-duty' from their respective Cliques, celebrating Fasnacht together with their offspring.

You'll see hundreds of children proudly wearing a proper costume, complete with mask and all. (Quite often, they use their creative talents and make their masks themselves out of old cardboard boxes.) As the afternoon wears on, many of the smaller kids take off their masks. After all, the wretched thing is not really that comfortable to wear. One has to get used to it by degrees.

That's how we learn about Fasnacht. We're brought up with it, infused with it at a very tender age. And once it has us in its grip, it never let's us go. Maybe that's why Tuesday afternoon is so magical. It's the cradle of Fasnacht.

Watching all these children with their families, you know that the tradition will continue – maybe not forever, but at least for another generation.

So let yourself be carried away. Follow the kids around town. Get behind one of these families. Maybe they'll take you all the way up to Münsterplatz. That's where, on Tuesday, the big lanterns are on show all day (and night). You really shouldn't miss that special show of art and humor.

Ladäärneusstellig (the lantern exhibition)

You could already admire the lanterns during Morgestraich or at Monday's parade as they appeared, passed you by and disappeared again in the distance. On Tuesday you can study them at leisure at the lantern exhibition. It is held in the big square surrounded by beautiful old buildings and the magnificent cathedral (Münster) built between 1185 and 1500. This provides a perfect background for an open-air art exhibition that is, once again, incomparable.

There are always about two hundred lanterns of different shapes and sizes on show. Each Ladäärne is made by stretching canvas around the outer walls of a cubic, wooden frame. The largest lanterns of the big Cliques (Stammvereine) are about three meters (10 feet) high and 1.5 meters (5 feet) wide, with a depth of 0.5 meters (2 feet). At night, they used to be lit by candles from the inside, but this is rarely seen today. Now they are lit from the inside by gas or electricity. You may wonder whether using gas isn't really too dangerous. Couldn't it burn? Well, anything burns, given the necessary amount of clumsiness. So don't worry. The people carrying them take the necessary precautions and know what they're doing. (The last incident I remember dates back to the 1980s. The fire was extinguished very quickly with no injuries. Even a large part of the lantern was saved.)

The painting on a lantern is closely linked to the theme or Sujet a Clique is presenting. The front usually captures the Sujet in one big cartoon that can easily be taken in from a distance. The back of the lantern narrates the theme in greater detail with small visual gags that are better viewed from close range. The name of the Clique and the title of the Sujet are found on the sides of the lanterns.

Looking closer, you see that, in addition to the painting, each lantern is covered with countless little verses, scribbled along the lines of the drawing. These are the so-called *Ladäärneväärs* (lantern verses), little puns of two-line commentaries about the painting that may surprise you with an unsuspected rhyme or twist. These verses are another important demonstration of Fasnacht humor.

Professionals, mostly commercial artists, usually paint the lanterns. Each has a different style which makes the lantern exhibition all the more interesting. Some lanterns are (or look) rather simple, others are quite elaborate. There's a lot of work in all of them. On average, a lantern painter needs about six weeks to complete it. And there is a lot of enthusiasm going into this art as well. But then, everything associated with Fasnacht involves enthusiasm.

Gugge

Tuesday is not only the day for children. It is also the day for *Guggemuusige*, generally known as *Gugge*. (Nobody seems to know why they are called this. The word means 'paper bag' in our local dialect.) We have already met these noisy musicians on Monday as a part of the parade. In fact, they are impossible to miss. They're big. They're loud. They're different.

A Gugge is, as I have mentioned before, a big brass band playing deliberately off-key. You may think that this is

Lifting the Mask

very easy, but it isn't quite as simple as that. A tune or a melody has to be recognisable. So if about 70 % of the band just blow away on their instruments, the rest of the band has to be all the more precise. The disharmony is planned and practised carefully. Sometimes, it takes months to get the sound just right.

Every Gugge (every good one anyway) has its own particular style of sound produced by a different conglomeration of instruments. One, for instance, is famous for including a couple of bagpipes. Another has piccolo players

Peter Habicht

in their midst. But the majority usually play brass instruments — trumpets, trombones, horns, tubas and the big sousaphones which always march at the end of the band. Sometimes, the instruments are old and crumpled with dents and scratches. And sometimes there are weird contraptions that aren't instruments at all but bizarre constructions made out of lids, stovepipes, hoses or whatever, provided a sound (= noise) can be made with it.

The rhythm is crucial. Every Gugge has traditional Basel drums, lots of other percussion instruments and at least two big kettledrums. They keep beating the rhythm even if the rest of the band isn't playing. The hard beat – so different from the rhythm of the 'traditional' Fasnacht drums – really gets under your skin. And when the rest of the Gugge band chimes in, every other sound, namely the drumming and piccolo melodies of the 'traditional' Cliques, is drowned out.

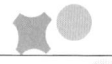

Sure enough, the members of the Cliques don't like this. It's one of the reasons why Gugge are not exactly loved by the rest of the active Fasnacht community. Some even say they're the black sheep of the family because they do all the things we were taught not to. Some of them tend to drink a lot (whereas you'll rarely see a drummer or piccolo player drunk because then they wouldn't be able to play their instruments well enough). Sometimes, the Gugge musicians even take their masks off when performing. What a sacrilege!

At best, Gugge are mildly tolerated. "They're OK," most of us would say, "there are just too many of them." Indeed, their numbers have increased in the last twenty or thirty years. Although the first Gugge appeared in the 19th century, they remained a rare exception until well after World War II.

In spite of the criticism, the Gugge enjoy an enormous popularity among the spectators. People follow them around in the streets and cheer when they perform in the restaurants (mainly on the 'other' side of the Rhine, in Kleinbasel). When, on Tuesday evening, the Gugge give their open-air concerts, their fans are packed in like sardines at Marktplatz, Barfüsserplatz and Claraplatz. A huge crowd moves to the rhythms of the crazy, swinging music – a music that contrasts so much to the grave solemnity of the traditional drums and piccolos. The Gugge are entertaining, cheerful and fun. No matter what the purists in the 'traditional' Cliques may say, the Gugge do add an indispensable element to the Fasnacht magic.

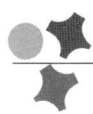

Wednesday

On Wednesday afternoon, there's a big parade again. It is just the same as Monday's – but maybe you haven't had enough of it. So have another look!

If you happen to hang around near Barfüsserplatz, you may observe a group of gentlemen (and ladies) in elegant dark suits, wearing rather old-fashioned hats with which they pompously salute the parading Cliques. They are the members of Fasnacht's organizing board called the Comité.

Organizing Fasnacht: the Fasnachtscomité

The Comité consists of 10 to 15 board members. It was founded in 1911 with the specific goal to organize Fasnacht and promote the interests of the Cliques, to uphold tradition and "to combat any 'un-Fasnacht-like' activity". True to its principles, it is a **very** conservative body. But things are changing even here. Only recently have they finally accepted women on their board. This was indeed a controversial matter. Ironically, the most important question seemed to be what kind of a hat a woman should wear during the parade. And should she take it off to salute the cliques? Well – these women do wear a hat. But they don't take it off as their male Comité members do.

It's a sport to make fun of the Comité. But on the whole, most people acknowledge that its members are doing a good job. The Comité organises not only the parade, but also big drum and piccolo concerts called *Drummeli* during the month before Fasnacht. At the parades on Monday and Wednesday, they are not just standing there being pompous. They judge the quality of the Cliques' processions and count the number of participants in each. According to the data they collect, they hand out subsidies to the Cliques, the Gugge and wagons (Wääge). These subsidies don't cover all the costs, but without them, the outstanding feats of these groups would not be possible.

Where does the money come from? The Comité raises it by selling a metal badge, the *Blaggedde*. There's a new one every year and it is usually very pretty – like a brooch with a nice Fasnacht motif. Everybody wears it visibly - the participants on their costumes, the spectators on their coat lapels. To have one is really a must. You can get it everywhere: at the kiosks, from street vendors or at your hotel. It comes in copper, in silver or in gold (that is, silver plated or gilded) and costs between 7 and 45 Swiss francs. By buying a Blaggedde, you help to keep the tradition of Fasnacht alive. Besides, it does make a nice souvenir.

The Comité doesn't just hand out the money, of course. It has certain requirements where the quality is

Lifting the Mask

concerned. Looking back on the history of Fasnacht (see page 75), this is probably its most important contribution. Right from its beginning, the Comité set a quality standard, a standard that is widely accepted, regardless of how much the board's decisions are derided or disputed (yet another Fasnacht tradition). It is largely due to this small board of organizers that Fasnacht has become what it is today.

Wild Fasnacht

Not every Fasnächtler takes part in the 'official' Fasnacht as organized by the Comité. In fact, only about half of the Fasnacht community does. The other half won't appear in official events like the parades on Monday and Wednesday. These unofficial Fasnächtler are called the 'wild' ones. But don't be afraid. They are not going to bite you. 'Wild' is meant to be the opposite of 'organized'.

I, for one, have never been in an official Clique. Wild Fasnacht is the form I know and like best. For many years, I went on my own. This is generally considered to be the hardest. You have to elbow your way through the crowd without a Vordraab to help you clear the way. You have to know your marches pretty well. If you miss a note or play off key, everybody notices (those are the moments you're really glad you wear a mask). On the other hand, you are your own master. You can choose your own itinerary and timetable. And you can play the tunes you like (instead of having to play the old boring ones all over again). Especially late at night these tunes sound great when you are alone in one of those tiny lanes where the big Cliques never go. The sound resonates from the walls of the old houses surrounding you. Then, it's just you, your piccolo – and the town you love so well. (Maybe this is my personal answer to the question about what Fasnacht is: it's a declaration of love).

They say only the best go on their own like this. I've never belonged to the best. I just didn't mind occasionally hitting a wrong note. But I had to practice a lot. And it's not always fun being alone in a big crowd, so when friends of mine started learning the piccolo a couple of years ago, I stopped going on my own. Together, we form one of those groups generally known as *Schyssdräggziigli*.

Schyssdräggziigli

You don't want to know what that means. Or do you? Well - *Schyssdrägg* is the four-letter-word starting with an 's' that I was taught not to use. One of its many meanings in our local dialect is 'triviality'. *Ziigli* is the diminutive of *Zug*.

Lifting the Mask

Literally, a Schyssdräggziigli is 'a small platoon of no importance'. Not a nice word, if you think about it. It was coined when – back in the 1960s – wild Fasnacht was unusual. Nowadays, it is a very popular (and important) form. And the word Schyssdräggziigli has survived. Everybody loves it – especially the members of the Schyssdräggziigli themselves. Perhaps only real Baslers can pronounce it correctly.

Basically, a Schyssdräggziigli is not so different from a Clique. (I'll probably get lynched for this). I mean, the things we do are the same. We also march around in our

Peter Habicht

costumes and play the traditional music. Only our bands are much smaller, and less structured and organized. There's room for spontaneity. If we run into a couple of friends we can join them for a round of marches around town. We can linger in a restaurant when a Schnitzelbangg arrives. We don't have to run out like the Cliques when their departure is scheduled. In a Schyssdräggziigli, you can do things according to your heart's desire.

There are hundreds of Schysdräggziigli, each one different. There are small ones with only two to four piccolo players and drummers. Others are larger, with ten to fifteen or more musicians. Some have a name (often meant to be cute or funny), others hold that a name is the first step towards becoming a Clique and having a cashier and board meetings and all that stuff. There are some small bands of highly-skilled piccolo musicians who have left their Cliques because they prefer to play all the fancy marches nobody else knew. And you'll find the musically less gifted struggling through their repertoire of evergreens.

What's also different is the amount of time and energy the members of a Schyssdräggziigli are ready to invest in the preparation of Fasnacht. Some make new costumes every year, costumes that are much more elaborate than the platoon-costume of the Cliques. Others just grab the same old outfit year after year and go out and have fun. The only thing all Schyssdräggziigli have in common is that they don't march in the parade which means they don't get any money from the Comité.

The Schyssdräggziigli I'm in will give you a picture of how things work. We're fairly average: middle aged, middle-class, and middle sized. We're a group of about 10 Pfyffer, a varying number of Vordraab and no drummers. (This is typical, too: the vast majority of wild Fasnächtler are piccolo-players.) We start preparing Fasnacht rather late in the year. We only get together in autumn to discuss whether we want to learn new marches or just go along with the old repertoire. Since we're a bit lazy, that's what we usually do. From then on, we meet weekly to rehearse and chat. We're not just 'doing' Fasnacht together, but we've become good, close friends. The social side of Fasnacht is one of its most important features.

In our group, this seems to become ever more important as we get on in life. The restaurant stops during Fasnacht get longer and longer every year. There are so many people to meet! We run into friends, for instance, who have moved away and only come back to Basel for these three days. So we sit around, sip our white wine (the standard Fasnacht beverage) and exchange news. But don't get me wrong! Every now and then, we grab our instruments and go out in the streets for another round of marching. We march along at random, playing our tunes up and down the hills of the old city center according to no prescribed route. We just go where our Vordraab takes us. There's a word for this way of enjoying Fasnacht - *gässle*.

Gässle

Gässle is a verb that exists only in our local dialect. It's derived from *Gasse* (lane) and can be translated as 'to hit the lanes'. Once again, the translation is highly inadequate. You have to experience it before you really understand its meaning. Gässle is not only marching around with drums and piccolos (or strolling behind those who do so). Gässle is a feeling, sometimes even a physical experience. The slow marching pace gets under your skin. (Long after Fasnacht you can observe people walking around in Basel at a rather peculiar gait.) Your whole body resounds with the beating of the drums and the piccolos' melodies. But not only your body. The entire city is vibrating like the soundbox of a huge instrument. That's what gässle is. With our instruments, we fill every street, every lane and hidden backyard with a cluster of sound. It's the favorite activity of most Fasnächtler. If you ask me, gässle is what Fasnacht is all about.

Not only the active Fasnächtler do it. You, as a spectator can do it too when you walk in step behind the bands. It's a great way to discover this city. Just follow any of the Cliques and Schyssdräggziigli around and explore Basel's medieval center with its little squares and narrow lanes and byways. Just pick one of the clusters of sound or rhythm you like, get in step and follow where your ears take you. Don't be afraid you might get lost. As long as you can hear the music, you're not far from the city center.

Those readers who have not yet experienced the Basel Fasnacht might be glad to have a few suggestions about where it's best to go. The old town (on the left-hand side of the Rhine) is built on two not-too-high hills. Above the river is the Münsterhügel with the cathedral and late medieval and baroque palaces. From the platform behind the church you have a wonderful view over the river to Kleinbasel ('little' Basel) and the Black Forest in the distance. From here you can amble downhill to Marktplatz with its magnificent Rathaus (City Hall, from the 16th century) and on to Barfüsserplatz, that owes its name to the old Franciscan church that dominates the square (Barfüsser = barefoot friars). Two shopping streets, Gerbergasse and Freie Strasse, connect Marktplatz and Barfüsserplatz. From Barfüsserplatz or Marktplatz, smaller lanes rise steeply towards St. Leonhards Church and St. Peters Church. This is the gothic part of town. The houses along Heuberg and Nadelberg date back to the 14th and 15th centuries. And don't miss seeing the Spalentor, a medieval city gate that is considered to be one of the finest historical monuments of Switzerland.

This is the main area where gässle takes place. There is some activity on the other side of the Rhine too. Try, for instance in the afternoon, the lovely promenade along the river between the Mittlere Brücke (the Middle Bridge) and the Wettsteinbrücke (Wettstein Bridge). On Monday and Wednesday evenings, Kleinbasel ('little'

Lifting the Mask

Basel) is where the Gugge play in the pubs and restaurants, whereas the Drummler and Pfyffer usually stay in Grossbasel ('big' Basel).

Where to go is really a matter of taste and preference. If you like bustling activity with a lot of big Cliques marching around, Rümelinsplatz is a good place to hang around. From here, walking up Spalenberg, you can start exploring the gothic part of town. It is much more romantic uphill, because the larger Cliques don't often go there. Or you can stroll towards the Hauptpost (main post office; very busy) and up the other hill (find the small lane called Schlüsselberg) towards the cathedral. Münsterplatz, of course, is very busy on Tuesday during the lantern exhibition. It is much more peaceful on Monday and Wednesday. But it's always worthwhile to come here and have a short break at the Pfalz (the platform overlooking the Rhine behind the cathedral). You won't stay there for long, as it is usually pretty cold and windy and there are not many restaurants nearby. So downhill you go, towards Barfüsserplatz or Marktplatz, back to where the action is.

Don't miss Andreasplatz. This charming square, hidden behind Schneidergasse, is the heart of 'wild' Fasnacht. Many Schyssdräggziigli meet to start their rounds here or have a break and a chat with friends before they go on another tour again.

The End

For three days, there's been plenty to do and see from early afternoon till (very) late at night (or more precisely until early in the mornings). On Monday and Tuesday nights, most people go home by 2 or 3 a.m. But no active Fasnächtler would dream of doing so on Wednesday.

The End is near! So everybody tries to make the most of the few remaining hours, minutes, seconds. On Wednesday night and early Thursday morning, Fasnacht reaches its climax.

The trance experienced by the active Fasnächtler the last three days and nights doesn't always work on the spectators. After midnight on Wednesday, people in plain clothes are getting rare. During the last hours of Fasnacht you'll see mostly the insiders. And for us, the Fasnächtler, the excitement gets more intense. Our restaurant breaks get shorter and shorter as the final hour draws closer. For the last round of music, we pick our favorite tunes. For playing the very last one, we pick a nice spot where we stand in a circle rather than march. And then the church bells strike 4 a.m. Everything must stop.

All of a sudden, it is quiet and calm again. Your ears still ring, but the noise that filled the city for three days has disappeared. Everybody takes off his or her mask, sighs deeply, says "*s'isch scheen gsi*" (it was beautiful) and heads to a restaurant for breakfast.

In the meantime, a legion of street-cleaners get to work. There are hundreds of brooms and huge modern street sweeping vehicles everywhere, their orange lights flashing, clearing away tons and tons of confetti and Zeedel (sometimes ankle deep) and piles of rubbish. It's a depressing sight for a Fasnächtler. After two hours of very hard work by the hundreds of men (mostly immigrants) hired for this job, the city is back to being as prim and proper as always. Nothing reminds you of the magic that took over the city of Basel for the last three days and nights. Fasnacht is over.

There is a kind of afterthought, however. On one of the three Sundays after Fasnacht, each Clique and Gugge celebrates what is known as a *Bummel*, a day's excursion to some neighbouring town or village where they eat, drink and play their Fasnacht tunes. They return to the center of Basel in the evening and march around town for a couple of hours. But they do this Bummel in their street clothes, not costumes. There are no lanterns, no Zeedel, no confetti. Although we enjoy this tradition, a Bummel isn't Fasnacht. It is only the echo. After that, we have to wait another year again.

Peter Habicht

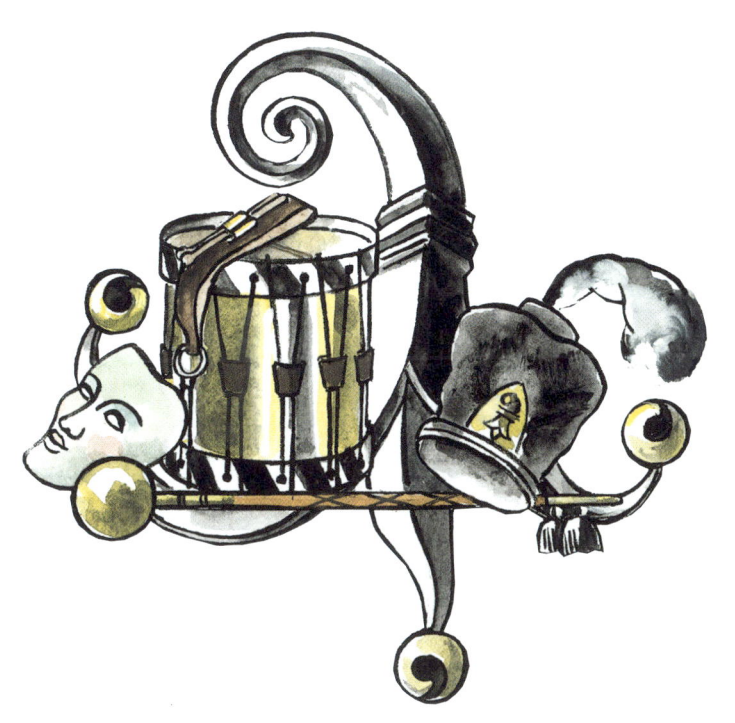

History

Fasnacht is an old lady. We call her lovingly 'Frau Fasnacht'. And we tend to cheat about her age, making her much older than she actually is. Some people point to the medieval roots and give you the impression that there has always been some kind of carnival in this city. It's a nice thought. But it's wrong. Fasnacht as celebrated today is only about 80 years old.

Some customs, like the drumming or wearing of masks do indeed have medieval roots. But the drumming wasn't necessarily associated with carnival in those days. And masks were re-introduced as late as the 1890s. The history of Fasnacht is a story of import and transformation. It has a lot to do with the way the city and its society has developed. But let's start with the two features that are truly medieval: the name and the date.

Medieval carnival was closely linked to the church calendar, namely the Lent period before Easter. The word derives from the Latin *carnem levare*, to take away the meat. The German word *Fastnacht* (in Switzerland, we omit the 't' in the middle of the word) is composed of *fasten* (to fast) and *Nacht* (night) and means 'the Eve of Lent'. In those days, it wasn't just meat that was forbidden. For more than a month, Christians weren't supposed to eat eggs or dairy products like butter or cheese. Small wonder that everybody packed in as much food (and fun) as possible before that.

Medieval carnival was a festival of abundance. People would eat, drink and have sex, all in excess it seems. There was merrymaking in various forms. A very popular motif was a 'world upside down'. Men would dress up as women, women as men. Often, they painted their faces with charcoal and wore masks. Social traditions or church rites were reversed. We read of fool kings or fool bishops reading blasphemous masses. Every town or village had its own tradition. In some places, old pagan rites to drive away winter were mixed in, which is understandable since spring wasn't far away when Lent began.

But when did Lent begin? Apparently, there was no unity of doctrine about that, although the period of fasting always lasted 40 days. Most towns followed Rome's lead, where the Sundays weren't considered to be days of fasting. Lent, therefore, started on Ash Wednesday. In a few places, people were fasting on Sundays as well. The Lent

Lifting the Mask

period started a week later – and so did carnival. The people of Basel were among the latter. In 1470, for example, the Lord Bishop invited guests to a sumptuous meal on a day when, in the neighbouring towns, everybody was already regrettably eating fish. Centuries later, when Fasnacht was re-vitalized, it had no connection whatsoever to church rites like fasting. But the unusual date was remembered. This is one of the reasons why Basel Fasnacht takes place a week later than in other places.

Carnival in the Middle Ages could turn quite violent. During this time of excess, social conflicts could escalate. In Basel, two such incidents are recorded. In 1376, a growing tension between the city's nobility and the guilds, who were gaining political influence throughout the 14th century, came to a clash. The riots that broke out during a tournament are still remembered as the *Böse Fasnacht* (evil carnival).

The carnival of 1529 also took place in a highly tense atmosphere. It was a time of great political upheavals. Only eight years before, the bishop had lost forevermore his position as sovereign. There was a power struggle between

Peter Habicht

the guilds and the patricians. Moreover, the question of the church reform that divided the city's population came to a climax. On February 9th, a band of (mostly) young men stormed the cathedral, tore out the altars and burned them on the square. This iconoclasm marked the victory of the Reformation in Basel. But it also marked the end of medieval carnival.

The reformers made short shrift with Fasnacht. Protestantism doesn't really encourage people to have fun. In Catholic areas carnival didn't last either. It was tamed in the days of the Counter-Reformation and finally disappeared. Nowhere is there an unbroken tradition of carnival from the Middle Ages. Our modern carnival is the result of a revival in the 19th century, a revival that happened only in Catholic areas. With one big exception: Basel.

At the end of the 18th century, Basel was a small town of about 25,000 inhabitants. It was politically, economically and socially dominated by the guilds of merchants and craftsmen who had established themselves after the Reformation. In the 19th century, industrialization set in, the population increased rapidly and finally exploded. By 1900, Basel had 109,000 inhabitants. Immigrants had come mainly from southern Germany and from other parts of Switzerland. Many of them were Catholics. They found it hard to become accepted in the city. Until 1875, they were denied all political rights. Also socially, the local establishment remained closed to outsiders. The immigrants started forming their own clubs and creating their own festivities.

They created Fasnacht. Or, more precisely, they took over a local tradition and started to transform it. The field was not quite barren. Throughout *Frühe Neuzeit* (16th to 18th century) the guilds had continued the (medieval) tradition of holding a big banquet on Ash Wednesday. In the late 18th century, these banquets were followed by mask and costume balls (*Maskenbälle*) and charades.

In the following week, on Fasnacht Monday and Wednesday, the guilds and corporations staged parades for the (male) youth. They resembled military parades. The boys dressed up as officers and soldiers (according to the social ranks of their fathers) and marched about town with rifles, playfully shooting in the air. They were accompanied by drums and fifes. The parades weren't particularly carnival-like. They were organised by the authorities and expressed symbolically the affiliation of the boys to the respective corporations and to the city's political system. These parades provided the platform from which Fasnacht would develop.

1833 was a black year for the city. After a rebellion in the countryside that nearly ended in civil war, the canton of Basel was divided into Basel-Stadt and Basel-Land. In the depression that followed, the establishment wasn't in the mood to celebrate. The balls and parades were dropped. They reappeared in the 1840s, but with a marked difference. The festivities weren't an exclusively upper-class event any longer. On the contrary! More and more immigrants started not only participating, but also organizing them, while the old families withdrew entirely.

With the immigrants taking over, things began to change. The newcomers introduced new elements they had brought with them from their native cantons and countries. In the 19th century, Fasnacht wasn't at all like it is today. Many immigrants came from north of the border and they wanted to celebrate pretty much in the same way as done at the carnivals in German Catholic towns. (There was, for instance, a 'Prince Carnival' preceding the parade on horseback. This was dropped in the beginning of the 20th century.)

On the whole, Fasnacht became funnier, without quite losing its military character as far as the music is concerned. Satirical poems were handed out. There was a larger variety of costumes too. In the 1840s, painted lanterns instead of torches were carried around at Morgestraich. Twenty years later, they appeared in the parades as well and soon became a major attraction. In 1876, a band played humorous "futuristic music". This is, without doubt,

After the painting by Hieronymus Hess 1842.

the first mention of a Guggemuusig; however, they remained a rare exception until well after World War II. In the 1890s the first masks were to be seen. They were made out of wax and didn't necessarily cover the whole face. Later, they were transformed to the characteristic masks you will see at Fasnacht today.

One by one, all the different 'ingredients' of Fasnacht have been introduced and either integrated or rejected. By 1920 the special blend of traditions was ready. In the meantime, the immigrants of the 19th century had formed a new and politically strong middle class. They successfully declared their festival to be a typical aspect of Basel, a part of the city's identity. To further this, all likeness to other forms of carnival was discouraged and the local dialect became the only accepted form of verbal expression. And slowly but surely, the old families, who had long scorned the 'amusement of the mob', joined in again.

It is only after World War I that Fasnacht became the festival everybody, regardless of religion and social status, could (and can) identify with. Today, you can find a multinational company's director and a factory worker side by side in the same Clique. And don't be surprised if a complete stranger addresses you in the informal *Du* form of 'you' (instead of the formal *Sie*). For three days, some formalities of everyday life are dropped.

Fasnacht was a much smaller affair back in the 1920s. Women, for instance, were excluded from marching in the streets. However they did appear in the highly popular masked balls, which have disappeared. The economic depression of the 1930s made it difficult to carry out the Fasnacht traditions. And World War II was certainly not a

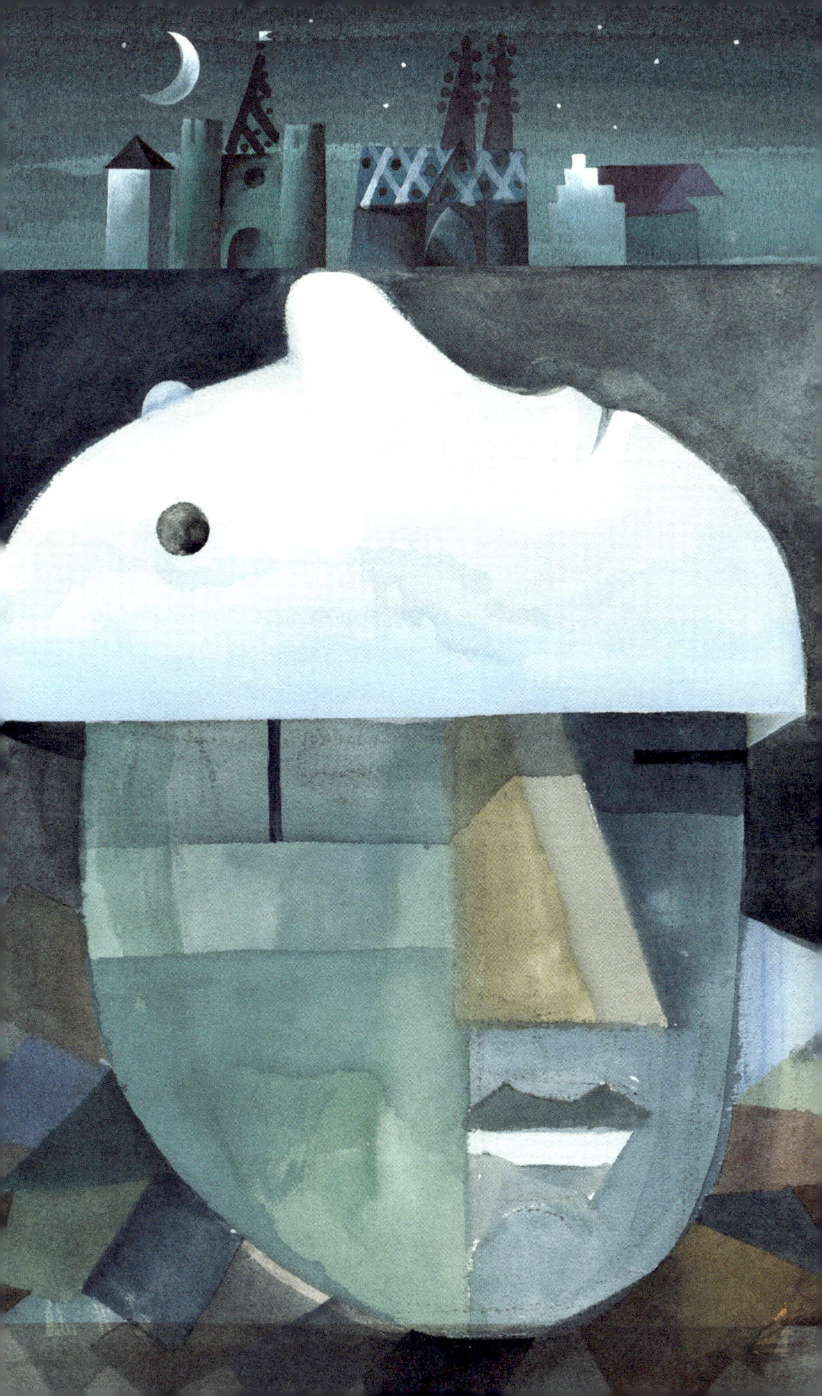

time for merrymaking. Fasnacht was suspended for six years. But once the dark clouds had blown away, the people of Basel wanted some fun and Fasnacht provided an ideal and creative platform. Elderly Fasnächtler today still refer with sparkling eyes to the Fasnacht of 1946 as 'the Fasnacht of the century'.

Since then, Fasnacht has evolved and been celebrated every year. Today it is a major event with more than 20,000 participants, attracting hundreds of thousands of visitors to Basel every year from far and wide.

Fasnacht is not only constantly growing but also changing. These changes may be difficult to spot at first and not so easy to describe. But when we look back, we recognize that the only consistent element of Fasnacht is that it changes with the times. It has to be like that. Fasnacht as a living tradition is a mirror of our society. New generations will produce new and different forms.

Maybe Fasnacht is best compared to the old mythological bird, the Phoenix. It shines in all imaginable colors. It burns in a consuming fire for three days – and then must die. But it will always rise out of the ashes. Forever new. Forever beautiful.

At a glance

Do's and don'ts

Carnival in general is a world turned upside down. To a certain degree, this is true for the Basel Fasnacht, too. But never forget it takes place in Switzerland! Fasnacht's first law is order, not chaos. There are many (unwritten) rules. Most of them are for the active Fasnächtler themselves, so they needn't bother you. There are, however, certain rules that you, as a visitor and spectator, should know and respect.

Buy a Blaggedde and wear it visibly on your coat.

This metal badge which has a new Fasnacht motif each year is issued by the Comité. The proceeds from its sale is handed out to the participating groups and helps to cover a part of their enormous costs. Think of buying a Blaggedde as your admission fee to a 72-hour performance. You've spent more money on worse shows. The Blaggedde come in four versions – copper for 8 francs, silver for 15 francs, gold for 45 francs, and a 'Bijou' for 100 francs. You can get them from many places the days before and during Fasnacht – from vendors calling out "Blaggedde" in the shopping streets of Basel, from the Basel Tourism office at Schifflände, and from kiosks and hotels.

Don't block the way

The masks worn and instruments played block not only a Fasnächtler's vision, but also his or her freedom of movement. Please don't stand in their way. People in masks and costumes always have the right-of-way. If there is a costumed group coming towards you, step aside. If you want to cross the street, wait until the whole procession of a Clique's piccolo players, drum major and drummers, have passed. Don't try to cross through the gap between drummers and pipers or their drum major.

Don't use a flash when taking photographs

Be sure to buy enough film beforehand because most of the shops are closed on Monday and Wednesday of Fasnacht. If you want to photograph (or film) Morgestraich, be sure that you **never use a flash**! By using a flash on your camera, you'll not only get a bad photograph but you kill the atmosphere of Morgestraich. And the flash from cameras is more than a nuisance for the costumed participants. They peep into the darkness through the tiny holes of their masks and a sudden flash of light blinds them for minutes. With a light-sensitive film you'll be able to get some fantastic pictures. If your camera flashes automatically, please leave it at home. Thank you!

No fireworks, please!

Some visitors seem to think that they can brighten things up with fireworks and crackers. They're in the wrong film. Fireworks only kills the atmosphere. Please don't use them.

Leave your fake nose at home

There's a strict division between those who participate actively as Fasnächtler and those who are onlookers only. To save you embarrassment, I recommend you leave your fake nose and your silly hat at home and don't paint your face. And drunken behavior won't make you very popular.

Dealing with confetti and pranks

Confetti is called *Räppli* in Basel. At times you may be ankle deep in confetti in the streets, but don't pick it up. You can purchase bags of confetti from stands around town. And please instruct your children not to throw confetti at the masked and costumed Fasnächtler. The confetti gets into their masks, eyes, noses, mouths and into their instruments. If a Waggis plays a prank on you, throws oranges at you or showers (or stuffs) you with confetti, please try to grin and bear it with magnanimity. Don't throw anything back.

Lifting the Mask

More hints

· Plan your visit to Basel at Fasnacht well in advance as hotels are always booked up then. If you are too late, try booking a room in another Swiss city like Bern or Zurich, or over the border in Germany or France. Check for special railway tickets and timetables that get you to Basel in time for Morgestraich from other cities around Switzerland.

· Do come early to Morgestraich. Basel is packed with people and you find yourself in an impenetrable crowd. Once Morgestraich has started, in some popular squares and streets you may find yourself squeezed in a mass of people that is moving in a direction you had not intended to go. Stay calm. It is advisable to agree beforehand upon a meeting point with your companions, as you can easily get separated from them.

· If you plan to bring your children, bear in mind that baby carriages and prams cause accidents (they cannot be seen in the crowds). If you can't carry small children on your shoulders, for their sake, it's best not to take them with you to Morgenstraich. During the parade, you should beware of the dangers to children who are looking for candy in the confetti along the route of the Waggis wagons. If your child gets separated from you in the crowd, stay calm. Lost children are well cared for at the police stations. When you frantically show up there you may find your little treasure happily devouring ice cream and sweets.

· Beware of pickpockets. They're out in numbers and enjoying a successful party, of course. Only they will notice your jewelry or your expensive watch. So leave valuables at home. Don't carry too much money with you and distribute it among several pockets. It's advisable not to carry hand or shoulder bags or backpacks with outside pockets.

What to eat

At Morgestraich, everybody eats *Määlsuppe* (flour soup) and *Ziibelewaije* (onion tart). If you feel you can't stomach this, try *Kääskiechli* (a savoury cheese tart). If you want a sweet (maybe in the afternoon), try the traditional *Fasnachtskiechli* (Fasnacht's cake). These are very thin, crispy pancakes covered with icing sugar. They're delicious (and of course fattening).

There's another speciality. Shortly before, during and after Fasnacht, the Basel bakers make special pretzels called *Faschtewaije*. They are covered with caraway seeds and can be highly recommended as snacks between meals.

All the restaurants are open until very late in the night (some don't close at all). In the evening, you need a lot of patience to get a table. But nobody has starved yet. During Fasnacht, the prices of food and drinks are often higher than usual. This isn't the fault of the waiters and waitresses. Their job is a hard one indeed. Although service charges are always included in restaurants in Switzerland, it is a thoughtful gesture to give the waiters and waitresses at Fasnacht a special tip (10% recommended).

If you want to make some Fasnacht delicacies yourself, I can highly recommend the following recipes by Sue Style.

Basler Määlsuppe

One of the classics of Fasnacht, this robust soup is just what's needed at 4 a.m. on a winter morning. If you can be bothered to make a good meat stock, the soup will be immeasurably better for it. Otherwise use 2 stock cubes and 1½ liters (6 cups) of boiling water. The soup can be prepared a day or two ahead, and even improves in flavor.

Serves 4

4 level tablespoons flour
50g (4 tbsp) butter
1 small onion, finely chopped
1 ½ liters (6 cups) meat stock
salt and pepper
a pinch of nutmeg
optional: 2-3 tablespoons grated Gruyère cheese

Put the flour in a large, heavy-based saucepan and set it over moderate heat. Let it turn a rich nut-brown, but be careful it doesn't burn. Remove from the heat and add the butter. Let it melt, and stir it into the flour to make a smooth paste. Return the pan to the heat and add the onion. Allow to cook for 5-10 minutes until the onion also takes a little color. Add the stock and bring to the boil, stirring energetically with a wire whisk to ensure no lumps form. Season to taste with salt, pepper and nutmeg and simmer for 30-40 minutes over low heat.

To serve, ladle the soup into deep rustic bowls, sprinkle with grated cheese (if using) and serve with plenty of crusty bread.

Ziibelewaije

This wonderful onion tart is a favorite for a restorative breakfast at Fasnacht. Some recipes use a Béchamel base; this one is thickened with eggs and cream. By brushing the pastry with egg white, you give it a waterproof coating which prevents the bottom from going soggy. Another tip is to start the tart off on the bottom of the oven, using bottom heat only (if your oven has this option). Then move it up to the middle of the oven to finish cooking. The best quiche pans are black metal, with a removable base, available in Swiss supermarkets or kitchen shops.

Peter Habicht

Serves 4

250g shortcrust (basic pie) pastry
1 egg white
6 large onions (about 600g), sliced
25g (2 tbsp) butter
salt and pepper
nutmeg
1 level tbsp flour
250ml (1 cup) milk
250ml (1 cup) whipping (light) cream
3 eggs
optional: 75g lardons (bacon cubes)

Roll out the pastry to fit a 30 cm (12 inch) quiche pan. Brush the pastry with egg white and chill it.

Melt the butter in a large, heavy pan and add the onions. Season to taste with salt, pepper and nutmeg. Cover the pan and stew the onions gently until they are a rich golden color. Do not allow them to brown. This will take at least 30 minutes.

Stir in the flour and cook a few minutes more until the flour is well mixed in. Remove the onions from the heat. With a wire whisk or hand-held blender, mix together the milk, cream and eggs. Season to taste with salt and pepper. The tart can be prepared ahead up to this point, and all the components refrigerated.

Heat the oven to 200°C/400°F, using only bottom heat if your oven has this option. Put the shelf on the lowest rung of the oven and set a heavy baking sheet on it. Spoon the onions into the pastry-lined quiche pan and pour the creamy-egg mixture over them. Scatter the lardons on top, if using.

Put the quiche pan onto the baking sheet and bake it for 20 minutes in the lower part of the oven. Reduce the heat to 180°C/350°F and finish baking the tart for a further 10-15 minutes or until the top is golden brown, the lardons crispy and golden, and the creamy-egg mixture is set.

Serve the tart warm – it also reheats successfully. Give it 15-20 minutes in a 180°C/350°F oven, covering with foil if necessary to prevent the top browning too much.

Recipes © 2001 Sue Style, author of *A Taste of Switzerland*, Bergli Books, Basel

Glossary

aagfrässe; what every *Fasnächtler* is: enthusiastic or hooked. Translated literally, it means nibbled or gnawed; like a loaf of bread or cheese the mice have gotten to.

Alti Dante; a traditionally costumed Fasnacht figure. She's the parody of an old spinster with a thin pointed nose, wearing an old-fashioned hat and dress. (See illustration page 31.)

Blaggedde; the metal badge that Fasnächtler and onlookers alike wear either on the costume or on coat lapels. It comes in copper (7 francs), silver (14 francs) and gold (45 francs). It's a symbol of your 'entrance fee' for Fasnacht. You won't get any treats from the Waggis without one!

Blätzlibajass; a traditionally costumed Fasnacht figure. (See illustration page 32.)

Bummel; the all-day excursion of Cliques and Guggemuusige on the three Sundays after Fasnacht.

Chaise; [pronounced: shaise] only appears in the parades on Monday and Wednesday afternoons. It is an open carriage drawn by one or two horses and occupied by two or four masked figures handing out treats to spectators.

Cliques; large groups of drummers and pipers. They are the backbone of Fasnacht. A Clique is a club or association with year-round activities associated with Fasnacht (e.g. teaching and rehearsing of the music, deciding upon a theme and costumes, preparing the lantern, Zeedel, wagons and the parades). On Fasnacht every Clique 'plays' (lampoons) a Sujet. Their whole appearance is dedicated to this: the costumes of the musicians, the gigantic lantern and the Zeedel.

Comité; the organising board of Fasnacht.

Cortège; the official word for the big parades on Monday and Wednesday afternoons of Fasnacht.

Drummeli; evening shows with music (drum and piccolo) and Rahmestiggli organized by the Comité in the month before Fasnacht.

Drummle; the most traditional of all Fasnacht musical instruments: the drum

Drummler; drummer

Dummpeeter; a traditionally costumed Fasnacht figure. (See illustration page 33.)

Fasnächtler; anybody who takes part in the event. In our dialect, we don't distinguish between participants and spectators, but between 'active' and 'passive' Fasnächtler. To save you (and myself) from confusion I have only called those who are wearing a mask and a costume Fasnächler. (Notice that Fasnächtler is both the singular and the plural form of the noun.)

Gässle; the activity every Fasnächtler likes best. It could be translated as 'to hit the streets (or lanes)' and signifies marching slowly in step around town in random directions. Both participants and spectators do it, either by playing drums and piccolos or by following behind the bands.

Gosdyym (or *Goschdyym*); Fasnacht costume. It is only one part of the disguise. A costume always has a mask (*Larve*) to go with it.

Guggemuusig; [pronounced: gook-a-moo-sick] the short form is *Gugge*. They are big brass bands that play enthusiastically and deliberately off-key. Their crazy swinging sound contrasts refreshingly to the traditional marching music of the drums and piccolos.

Harlekin; a traditionally costumed Fasnacht figure. (See illustration page 32.)

Kopfladäärne; a small lantern fixed on top of a mask. You'll see them mainly at *Morgestraich*.

Ladäärne; the gigantic, artistically painted lanterns carried around by the Cliques. They light the darkness at Morgestraich. In the parades, they are the pride and centerpiece of the Clique's appearance. On Tuesday, all lanterns are exhibited at Münsterplatz (all day and all night). This lantern exhibition is not to be missed.

Larve; the Basel dialect word for a mask. Sometimes, we refer to it as *Kopf* (head) which shows its importance.

Marsch; almost the same word in English: a march. It's the traditional Fasnacht music as played by the drums and piccolos.

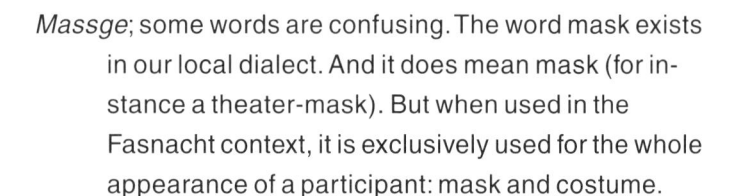

Massge; some words are confusing. The word mask exists in our local dialect. And it does mean mask (for instance a theater-mask). But when used in the Fasnacht context, it is exclusively used for the whole appearance of a participant: mask and costume.

Määlsuppe; the traditional Morgestraich menu: a soup of roasted flour, served with grated cheese (see recipe page 93).

Morgestraich; not only the beginning, but also the highlight of Fasnacht. This magical moment at 4 a.m. on a wintry Monday morning, this sudden explosion of music and colors is worth a journey (even a long one) to Basel. Morgestraich is also the name of a tune or march. It's the melody Fasnächtler play first thing when the streetlights go out and Fasnacht begins. It is an old assembly call of the Swiss army and thus an indicator of the origins of the tradition: a pre-dawn military tattoo or bugle-call.

Pfyffer; piccolo-player or piper.

Piccolo; besides the drum, this is the other traditional Fasnacht instrument. It is quite different from a concert piccolo. It is a shorter version of the traversal flute. The Basel piccolo has both keys and holes and is therefore easier to play.

Pierrot; a traditionally costumed Fasnacht figure. (See illustration page 33.)

Rädäbäng; a magazine edited by the *Comité* and available shortly before Fasnacht. It lists all the groups participating in the parade and the themes (*Sujets*) they are lampooning. The information is in dialect and the themes as given may not yet be evident even to the insider. You can buy a Rädäbäng for 8 francs at every kiosk. The funny looking word comes from the sound you make when you beat a drum with two drum sticks.

Rahmestiggli; a humouros sketch played in the *Drummeli* or similar events in the month before Fasnacht.

Räppli; the dialect word for confetti. The word is a diminutive form of the smallest Swiss coin, the *Rappen* (one Rappen equals a cent or 1/100th of a Swiss franc). But Räppli are certainly not as valuable as that, so

Lifting the Mask

don't pick them off the ground. They are not to be thrown at masked Fasnächtler.

Requisit; part of the *Zug*. It's a strange 'sculpture' composed of one or several objects artistically arranged on a small waggon.

Schnitzelbangg; [pronounced schnit-sell-bunk] the word for either a group of masked Fasnächtler singing funny verses in a restaurant – or for the verses themselves. It's a highly popular (and unique) art and poetry form and the most important demonstration of Basel Fasnacht humor. To appreciate fully the performances of the Schnitzelbänggler (plural form) one has to understand the local dialect. But their tunes, costumes and flip-chart art are delightful.

Schyssdräggziigli; [pronounced sheess-drag-zig-le] the small 'wild' bands of *Drummler* and *Pfyffer* (drummers and piccolo players) who are not part of the Comité and its organization. They do not march in the Cortège parades but whenever and wherever they want at random.

Stäggeladäärne; a small lantern carried on a pole.

Stange; [pronounced stang eh] is what you order when you want a beer. It's a bit more than half a pint and stronger than English or American beer.

Sujet; the subject or theme a Clique is lampooning. It is ever so important. The whole Fasnacht appearance of a Clique, including the lantern and the costumes of the musicians, is based on it each year.

Tambourmajor; the drum major. He is the most notable figure of the Zug with an enormous mask and a long staff with which he conducts the band.

Ueli; a traditionally costumed Fasnacht figure. (See illustration page 31.)

Vordraab; the vanguard. Vordraab are those members of the bands that do not play an instrument but who march in front of the musicians, clearing the way through the crowds. During the Cortège parades, they hand out the Clique's Zeedel.

Wääge; big wagons or floats from where, during the parades, the rowdy, fun-loving Waggis throw sweets, oranges, flowers and confetti to spectators.

Waggis; the best-known Fasnacht figure. He has a huge nose (and mouth) and a colorful straw mane. During the parade, he rides on the wagons or big floats. (See illustration page 30.)

Wysse; white wine: the standard beverage of Fasnacht. We drink a lot of it, but for most Fasnächtler, Fasnacht is not the time for drinking binges.

Zeedel; strips of paper, on which the Clique's Sujet is dealt with in a long satirical poem written in the local dialect. Zeedel are distributed to spectators as the Cliques march along.

Ziibelewaije; an onion tart especially enjoyed at Morgestraich. Very traditional and very tasty. (See recipe page 95.)

Zug; the entity of a Clique. It consists of Vordraab, Pfyffer, Tambourmajor and Drummler. Its centerpiece is the gigantic lantern. The word is of military origin and means a platoon.

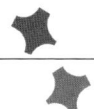

Bibliography

Back, Anita: *Basler Fasnacht*, Dortmund 1988.

Batschelet, Bernhard: *Die Musik der Basler Fasnacht*, in: Schibli, Sigfried: Musikstadt Basel, Basel 1999.

Blum, Dieter: *Basler Fasnacht: Menschen hinter Masken*; with texts by Dominik Wunderlin and Urs Ramseyer, Basel 1999.

Burckhardt-Seebass, Christine, Mooser Josef et al.: *Zwischentöne. Fasnacht und städtische Gesellschaft in Basel 1923-1998*. Basel 1998.

Meier, Eugen A. et al.: *Die Basler Fasnacht. Geschichte und Gegenwart einer lebendigen Tradition*, Basel 1985.

Sütterlin, Walter: *Fasnacht von A bis Z*. Photographs by Walter Süterlin, text by -minu, Basel 1994

Trachsler, Beat: *Basler Fasnacht: for Insiders and Outsiders*, Basel 2001

Internet addresses
   www.bsonline.ch
   www.vtour.ch
   www.fasnacht.ch
   www.fasnachts-comite.ch
   www.gugge-ig-basel.ch

Index

A

aagfrässe 7, 98
Alsatians 29
(die) Alte *see* marches
Altfrangg *see* costumes, *also* marches
Alti Dante *see* costumes
Alti Garde 40
Ash Wednesday 7, 77, 80

B

Bajass *see* Blätzlibajass
Basel, buildings
  Hauptpost 72
  Kunstmuseum 35
  Leonhardskirche 19, 71
  Martinskirche 19
  Münster 55, 71, 72, 79
  Peterskirche (St. Peters' church) 71
  Rathaus (City Hall) 71
  Spalentor 71
Basel humor 45–46
Basel, streets and squares
  Andreasplatz 72
  Barfüsserplatz 35, 61, 62, 71, 72
  Claraplatz 35, 61
  Freie Strasse 18, 71
  Gerbergasse 71
  Heuberg 71
  Kleinbasel 35, 61, 71
  Marktplatz 18, 35, 61, 71, 72

Mittlere Brücke 35, 71
Münsterhügel 71
Münsterplatz 72, 55, 101
Nadelberg 71
Pfalz 72
Rümelinsplatz 72
Schlüsselberg 72
Schneidergasse 72
Spalenberg 72
Steinenberg 35
Wettsteinbrücke 35, 71

Baseldytsch 8. *see also* dialect
Blaggedde 63, 87, 98
Blätzlibajass *see* costumes
Böse Fasnacht 79
brass bands *see* Guggemuusig
Bummel 74, 98

C

carnival 9, 10, 45, 51, 75-79, 87
Chaise 39, 99
Charivari 28
cheese tart 91
children 30, 39, 51–54, 89, 90
Clique 13, 20, 28, 39-44,
    51, 56, 60, 63, 65, 66, 84, 88, 101, 105, 106
Cologne 10
Comité 13, 62–64, 68, 87, 99
Commedia dell'Arte 26, 32, 33, 34
confetti 29, 39, 54, 74, 89, 103
Cortège 35–39, 99

costumes 12, 13, 14, 20, 31, 38, 40, 41, 51, 54, 63, 67, 68, 74, 80, 82, 88, 105
Costumes and masks 25–34
  Altfrangg 26
  Alti Dante 30–31, 39, 98
  Blätzlibajass 26, 32, 98
  Dummpeeter 34, 100
  Harlekin 26, 101
  Pierrot 34, 103
  Stänzler 26
  Waggis 29, 29–30, 38, 39, 89, 91, 98, 105, 106

D

dialect 7, 8, 9, 25, 29, 32, 42, 45, 57, 65, 69, 84
do's and don'ts 12, 87–89
Druggede 8
drum 12, 13, 15, 19-25, 38, 54, 60, 61, 63, 70, 80, 100
drum major *see* Tambourmajor
Drummeli 13, 63, 99
drumming 19, 20, 22, 40, 60, 70, 75
Drummle *see* drum
Dummpeeter *see* costumes

E

Easter 9, 41, 76

F

Faschtewaije 92
Fasnachtscomité *see* Comité
Fasnachtsfieber 13–14, 41

Fasnachtskiechli 91
fifes *see* piccolo
floats *see* Wääge
flour soup *see* Määlsuppe
flute *see* piccolo

G

Gässle 69–72, 100
Gugge *see* Guggemuusig
Gugge concerts 8, 61
Guggemuusig 8, 9, 12, 13, 38, 57–60, 72, 83, 98, 101
guild 22, 78, 79, 80
Güpfi 28

H

Harlekin *see* costumes
Helge 47, 50
horse-drawn carriages 39 *see* Chaise
hotels 90
humor 44–45, 57

I

Internet addresses 107

J

Jungi Garde 40

K

Kääskiechli 91
Karneval *see* carnival

Kopfladäärne *see* Ladäärne

L

Ladäärne
  Kopfladäärne 15, 101
  Ladäärne 15, 101
  Ladäärne yypfyffe 13
  Ladäärneusstellig 55
  Ladäärneväärs 56
lanterns 13, 15, 42, 45, 55, 55–57, 83. *see* Ladäärne
Larve 25, 101, *see* mask
Lent 10, 76–78
Lucerne 10

M

Määlsuppe 18, 91, 92, 102
Mainz 10
marches 24–25
  die Alte 24
  Altfrangg 26
  Arabi 24
  Barogg 24
  d'Brite 24
  s'Nunnefirzli 24
  Whisky 24
Mardi Gras 10
Marsch *see* marches
mask 12, 13, 14, 15, 25, 38, 41, 42, 47, 54, 60, 65, 73, 75, 76, 77, 80, 84, 88, 89, 100, 101, 102
Middle Ages 22, 31, 75, 78, 78–79, 79, 80
military marches 24

military roots 19, 22, 80
mimosas 39
Morgestraich 8, 15–18, 28, 38, 83, 88, 90, 91, 101
Morgestraich march 19
music 10, 13, 19–22, 24, 57–60, 73, 81, 99, 101, 102

N
New Orleans 10

O
onion tart 18, 91, 94, 106. *see also* Ziibelewaije
organization *see* Comité

P
Parade 8, 10, 18, 28, 30, 35–39, 40, 42, 46, 51, 55, 57, 62, 63, 64, 68, 80, 81, 82, 90
piccolo 9, 12, 13, 14, 19, 20, 21, 22, 22-23, 26, 39, 40, 58, 60, 63, 65, 67, 68, 80, 88, 99, 102, 103, 104
pickpockets 91
Pierrot *see* costumes
police 91
preparations 13, 41, 68

R
Rädäbäng 103
Rahmestiggli 13, 99, 103
Räppli *see* confetti
Recipes 93-97

Reformation 79
Requisit 42, 104
ridicule 31
Rio 10
Rule Britannia 24
rules 87–89

S

satire 44
Schnitzelbangg 13, 45, 46–50, 67, 104
Schyssdräggziigli 65–69, 70, 72, 104
Scotland the Brave 24
shops 35, 51
Stäggeladäärne 15, 104. *see also* Ladäärne
Stammclique 40
Stange 105
subsidies 63
Sujet 28, 38, 41, 42, 43, 43–44, 56, 99, 103, 105

T

taking photographs 88
Tambourmajor (drum major) 42, 88, 105, 106
themes *see* Sujet
topics *see* Sujet

U

Ueli *see* costumes

V

Väärs 47

Venice 10
Vordraab (vanguard) 15, 42, 64, 68, 69, 105

W

Wääge 38, 99, 105
Waggis *see* costumes
Waggiswääge 51
wagons *see* Wääge
where it's best to go 71–72
world upside down 76
Wysse 106

Z

Zeedel 41–42, 45, 47, 50, 74, 106
Ziibelewaije 91, 94, 106
Zug 42, 43, 65, 106

Acknowledgements

The publisher wishes to express sincerest appreciation to the following people who read the manuscript and provided many helpful comments about this book: Anne-Louise Bornstein, Clara von Deschwanden, Larry Desmond, Mary Hogan, Annette Keller, Angela Joos, -minu, Edith Schweizer-Völker, Annemarie Seiler, Carol Siegenthaler, Deirdre Smith and Martin Strauch, and others.

About the author and the illustrator

The author

Peter Habicht is a historian in Basel who enjoys giving lively, carefully researched tours of the town closest to his heart. Basel's Fasnacht may be impossible to describe, but Peter Habicht's tour in these pages is the next best thing to spending these three special days in Basel.

The artist

Fredy Prack is a graphic designer in Basel and one of the most valued artists for Fasnacht lanterns. He is well-known for conveying the themes, humor and heart of the Basler (and Schnitzelbänggler) into a visual form.

About Bergli Books

Bergli Books publishes, promotes and distributes books mostly in English that focus on living in Switzerland.

Ticking Along with the Swiss
Ticking Along Too
Ticking Along Free
Cupid's Wild Arrows -
    intercultural romance and its consequences
Laughing Along with the Swiss
Once Upon an Alp
Swiss Me
A Taste of Switzerland
Berne - a portrait of Switzerland's federal capital,
    of its people, culture and spirit
Beyond Chocolate - understanding Swiss culture
Hoi - your Swiss German survival guide
Culture Smart Switzerland - a quick guide to customs
    and etiquette
Ticking Along with Swiss Kids

A German edition of Lifting the Mask is available and has the title 'pfyffe ruesse schränze'.
Detailed information about all the Bergli publications can be found at www.bergli.ch.

Dear Reader

Your opinion can help us. We would like to know what you think of Lifting the Mask - your guide to Basel Fasnacht.

Where did you learn about this book?

Had you heard about Bergli Books before reading this book?

What did you enjoy about this book?

Any criticism?

Would you like to receive more information about the books we publish and distribute? If so, please give us your name and address and we will send you a catalog.

Name:
Address:
City/Country

Cut out page, fold here, staple and mail to:

Bergli Books
Rümelinsplatz 19
CH-4001 Basel
Switzerland